HANDING ON THE FAITH
IN AN AGE OF DISBELIEF

JOSEPH CARDINAL RATZINGER

with

ARCHBISHOP DERMOT J. RYAN (Dublin)
GODFRIED CARDINAL DANNEELS (Malines/Brussels)
FRANCISZEK CARDINAL MACHARSKI (Krakow)

HANDING ON THE FAITH IN AN AGE OF DISBELIEF

Lectures given at the Church of Notre-Dame
de Fourvière in Lyons, France
and at Notre-Dame Cathedral in Paris
With commentaries by Pierre Eyt, Bernard Bro, O.P.,
Georges Bonnet, and Jacques Guillet, S.J.

Preface by Jean-Marie Cardinal Lustiger and
Archbishop Albert Decourtray

Translated by Michael J. Miller

IGNATIUS PRESS   SAN FRANCISCO

Original French edition:
Transmettre la foi aujourd'hui
© 1983 by Coopérative de l'Enseignement Religieux de Paris
et Le Centurion, Paris

German edition:
Die Krise der Katechese und ihre Überwindung:
Rede in Frankreich
©1983 by Johannes Verlag, Einsiedeln
© Herder Verlag, Freiburg im Breisgau

Cover art © Corbis

Cover design by Riz Boncan Marsella

CONTENTS

INTRODUCTION

Of the four distinguished testimonials in Paris and Lyons (January 1983) concerning what is essential for a truly ecclesial catechesis in the countries of the West and of the Eastern bloc, only Cardinal Ratzinger's lecture met with displeasure, partly because he came from Rome, and partly because he candidly pointed out things that were still lacking in catechetical textbooks in France, despite many years of efforts to develop proper materials for religious instruction. The strange fascination exercised by Bultmann over French theology to this day (which was over in Germany by the early 1950s) is probably to blame for the failure to bridge adequately the "horrid trench" between the "historical Jesus" and the "Christ of faith".

In this German edition, Cardinal Ratzinger's lecture has a more prominent place and has been supplemented with an interview granted in Germany. This is on account of the recent salutary response [to the Cardinal's statements on both occasions] and is in no way intended to slight the presentations by the ordinaries of Dublin, Malines-Brussels, and Krakow.

It was a felicitous idea of the two editors of the French edition to have renowned theologians write reflection papers on the contents of all four of the lectures, and their enlightening commentaries are a welcome addition here as well.

This entire book is a fine example of what Saint Paul values so highly as ecclesial *paraklesis*: a fraternal reminder about what is essential to the faith and at the same time exhortation, encouragement, consolation, and all in the loving *communio* of the local Churches in the one Catholic Church.

Hans Urs von Balthasar
(Translator of the 1983 German edition)

FOREWORD

Will Christians of the twentieth century be able to hand on the good news that they themselves have received? This question weighs upon believers as a test of their faith. It is a challenge presented to the Church in the contemporary world.

The Second Vatican Council posed and dealt with this question of the transmission, the tradition of the faith (*Lumen gentium* and *Dei Verbum*) in the modern world (*Gaudium et spes*). The Synods on Evangelization (1974) and on Catechesis (1977) and the two documents that resulted from those gatherings—*Evangelii nuntiandi* (1975) and *Catechesi tradendae* (1979)—are proof enough that this concern did not disappear with the conclusion of the Council. Paul VI, John Paul I, and John Paul II deemed that this task called for consultation and collaboration with the bishops of the different Churches.

In the remarks he addressed to the French bishops of the region of Île-de-France during their *ad limina* visit in September 1982, John Paul II quoted *Catechesi tradendae*, saying, "You are beyond all others the ones primarily responsible for catechesis" (no. 63). Thus he reminded us that it is up to the bishop to watch over the integrity of this transmission of the faith and over the quality of the methods and resources that are applied.

We have to consider the questions posed by catechesis and its methods in light of this mission. We should evaluate within this same context the work accomplished in France over the past fifty years, in which the archdioceses of Lyons and Paris have distinguished themselves in turn.

Not all the fruits of these painstaking labors can be listed here; some of them, however, should be mentioned.

An ongoing pastoral effort has made it possible to extend catechesis over a longer period of years than previously, when it lasted only through the preparations for First Holy Communion. The contents of this catechesis benefited from the fruits of the biblical renewal and offers a more substantial introduction to Scripture than the [French] national Catechism of 1947.

Parents and numerous catechists have been recruited to catechize children. Many found that they were not prepared for the work entrusted to them. Without claiming that all the lacunae of an often inadequate formation have been filled, we can say that pioneers like Joseph Collomb, diocesan priests in charge of religious education, and consecrated religious have responded to the need for improved, effective training of catechists.

The work that has been undertaken has made everyone aware of the biblical and theological implications of all catechetical activity. All sorts of recent studies in both of these fields, of course, prevent us from being content with simplistic solutions. Then, too, we are still far from having drawn all the theological and pastoral conclusions from the major constitutions of Vatican II, especially *Lumen gentium, Gaudium et spes*, and *Dei Verbum*.

And so the task that lies ahead of us is still gigantic, and we expect much from the work of theologians and exegetes. This means, furthermore, that in catechesis, more than in any other field, there is an essential distinction between research into various catechetical, exegetical, and theological trends and the common teaching of the Church, as she must present it to her children.

For various reasons, the initiatives taken in France have had remarkable effects abroad. We are conscious of the responsibility we consequently have toward the other local Churches. Today, more than ever, we should carry on this work in a collaborative way, and not in isolation.

The international implications of the projects undertaken in France, the universal and thoroughly Catholic effect of catechetical activity, and the primary and immediate responsibility of the bishops in this area relegate reflections about catechesis and dogmatic and pastoral efforts for this cause to the province of episcopal collegiality, as it is manifested in the most recent period of Church history. We have given expression to the *communio* of the apostolic college by inviting the Prefect of the Congregation for the Doctrine of the Faith, who is a close collaborator of the Pope, as well as the Archbishops of Krakow, Malines-Brussels, and Dublin.

The papers presented here clearly show that each lecturer spoke according to his theological competence, his pastoral experience, and his personal background. No one will imagine that Dublin, Brussels, Lyons, and Paris face identical pastoral situations. No one, nevertheless, can restrict his catechetical approach to the special circumstances of his country.

Within the one Catholic Church, every particular Church is mystically and practically united with the other Churches of God. Their union within this *communio*—as it is traditionally called—is expressed in different ways, not only through relationships between the individual bishops, but also through the reception accorded by each Church to the experience of the others. At a time when international relations are being renewed and intensified, it would be paradoxical if our Catholic Church, which is universal by her vocation, were not in fact a place of ongoing exchange among her members.

In this spirit, Cardinals Ratzinger, Macharski, and Danneels and Archbishop Ryan accepted our invitation and presented to us their testimony, which we accepted as a pledge of *communio*.

Therefore we are especially pleased to present to French-speaking readers the texts of the lectures that were given last January [1983] at the Church of Notre-Dame de Fourvière [in Lyons, France], and at Notre-Dame Cathedral in Paris. In order to facilitate an understanding and analysis of them, we have asked four theologians to share their reactions to these papers. We thank them for contributing in this way to a better *communio* among the Catholic Churches of Europe.

Jean-Marie Cardinal Lustiger
Archbishop of Paris

Albert Decourtray
Archbishop of Lyons

Joseph Cardinal Ratzinger

Handing on the Faith and the Sources of the Faith

The last words that the risen Lord spoke to his disciples commissioned them to go out into all the world and to be his witnesses (Mt 28:19f.; Mk 16:15; Acts 1:8). An essential part of the Christian faith is the fact that it is meant to be handed on. It consists of coming to know a message that concerns everyone, because it is the truth and because man cannot be saved without the truth (1 Tim 2:4). Therefore catechesis, the transmission of the faith, has been a central vital function of the Church from the beginning and will necessarily remain one for as long as there is a Church.

I. The Crisis of Catechesis and the Problem of Sources

1. *General Description of the Crisis*

That catechesis is having a difficult time is a platitude that does not need to be demonstrated at great length. The reasons for the crisis and its consequences have been described often and extensively.[1] In the technological world, which is

---

[1] See the publications of the French Synod of Bishops and its counterpart in the German Federal Republic: Conférence épiscopale française, *La Catéchèse des enfants: Texte de référence* (Paris: Centurion, 1980), pp. 11–26; Gemeinsame

a self-made world of man, one does not immediately encounter the Creator; rather, initially, it is only himself that man always encounters. The fundamental structure of this world is feasibility, and the manner of its certainty is the certainty of what can be calculated. Therefore even the question of salvation is not geared to God, who appears nowhere; rather, once again, it is geared to the ability of man, who wants to become the engineer of himself and of history. Accordingly, he no longer seeks his moral standards, either, in discourse about creation or the Creator, since such talk has become unfamiliar to him. For him, creation is silent with regard to morality; it speaks only the language of mathematics, of technological utility, or else it protests against its violation by man. But even then its moral exhortation remains indeterminate; ultimately, in one way or another, morality becomes identified with social acceptability, compatibility with man and his world. In this respect morality, too, has become a question of calculating the best possible arrangement of the future. All of this has fundamentally changed society. To a great extent the family, the basic sustaining social form of Christian culture, is in the process of disintegrating. When metaphysical ties do not count, other sorts of commitment can scarcely shape it in the long run. This whole world view is mirrored, on the one hand, in the new media and, on the other hand, is nourished by them. To a great extent, the representation of the world and of events in the media today makes more of an impression on people's awareness than their own experience of reality. All of this affects catechesis, which finds that its traditional social supports—family and parish—are present only

Synode der Bistümer in der Bundesrepublik Deutschland, *Offizielle Gesamtausgabe* 1 (Freiburg, 1976), pp. 123ff.

in broken form. Since it can no longer connect with the
experience of faith lived out in the living Church, it seems
to be condemned to remain mute in an age whose language and thought feed almost exclusively by now upon
experiences of the self-made world of man.

Catechetics [*praktische Theologie*] has applied itself energet-
ically in recent decades to this set of problems, in order to find
new ways of handing on the faith that are adapted to this situation. In the meantime, admittedly, many have come to the
conclusion that these efforts, instead of helping to overcome
the crisis, have tended in large measure to aggravate the problems. It would be unfair to declare this as a generalization,
but it would also be dishonest to deny it completely. An initial and momentous error down this road was doing away with
the catechism and declaring in general that the literary genre
"catechism" was outmoded. Although it is true that the catechism, as a book, was not customary until the age of the
Reformation, nevertheless a basic structure for transmitting
the faith, developed from the logic of the faith, is as old as
the catechumenate, which is to say that it is as old as the
Church herself. It follows from the very essence of her commission and is therefore indispensable. The renunciation of a
structured, fundamental schema for transmitting the faith,
drawing upon tradition in its entirety, resulted in a fragmen-
tation of the faith presentation, which not only abetted arbi-
trariness, but also simultaneously called into question the
seriousness of the individual elements of the content, which
belong to a whole and, when detached from it, appear hap-
hazard and incoherent.

What was behind this hasty and wrong decision, which was
implemented internationally with great confidence? The reasons are multifaceted and as yet hardly investigated. First of
all, to be sure, there is a connection here with the general

didactic and pedagogical development that was characterized quite generally by a hypertrophy of method as opposed
to content. The method became the measure of the content
and was no longer the vehicle for it. "Supply is determined
by demand"—so the way of the new catechesis was described
in connection with the *Dutch Catechism*.[2] So the instructor
had to stop at what was immediately accessible, instead of seeking ways of going beyond it and advancing to things that are
not understood at first but that alone can make a positive
change in man and the world. In this way the actual potential of the faith to be an agent of change was crippled. Catechetics now understood itself, no longer as a continuation
and concretization of dogmatic theology or of systematic theology, but rather as a self-sufficient standard. This in turn cor-
responded to the new tendency to rank praxis over truth,
which within the context of neo-Marxist and positivistic phi-
losophies now made its way into theology as well.[3] All of this
overlapped with a far-reaching reductionism in anthropology: the priority of method over content means the priority
of anthropology over theology, which had to subordinate itself
to a radical anthropocentrism. With the collapse of anthropology, the center of gravity shifted and new emphases
appeared: the predominance of sociology or even the primacy of experience, which became the measure for one's
understanding of the faith heritage.

Behind these and other reasons that could be cited for
the repudiation of the catechism and the breakdown of classical catechesis, however, we must of course look for a process that goes deeper. The fact that catechists no longer

[2] See the evidence presented in J. Ratzinger, *Dogma und Verkündigung*
(Munich, 1973), p. 70.

[3] See J. Ratzinger, *Principles of Catholic Theology*, trans. Mary Frances McCar-
thy (San Francisco: Ignatius Press, 1987), pp. 309–11.

dared to present the faith as an organic whole, on its own terms, but only piecemeal, in excerpts that reflected individual anthropological experiences, was ultimately due to the fact that they no longer had confidence in that whole. It was due to a crisis of faith, or, more precisely, to a crisis of the faith shared *with* the Church of all ages. As a consequence, dogma was largely left out of catechesis, and teachers tried to construct the faith right out of the Bible. Now dogma is, in fact, essentially nothing other than the explanation of Scripture, but the explanation that had developed within the centuries-old faith no longer seemed quite compatible with the understanding of the texts that had been introduced in the meantime by the historical method. And so two apparently irreconcilable forms of interpretation now stood side by side: the historical interpretation and the dogmatic interpretation. The latter, when viewed through the prism of contemporary thought patterns, was deemed inadequate, an unscientific first step toward the new interpretation. And so it seemed difficult to acknowledge that it had a status of its own. When scientific certainty is regarded as the only permissible or the only possible form of certainty, then the certainty of dogma necessarily appears to be either an outmoded, archaic stage of thought or else the emanation of the will to power of self-perpetuating [*bestehender*] institutions. It should then be measured by the standard of scientific exegesis and can at best serve to corroborate the statements of the latter, although it can no longer judge them authoritatively.

2. *Catechesis, the Bible, and Dogma*

With that, however, we have arrived at the heart of the matter we are discussing, since it is a question of the status of the "sources" in the process of handing on the faith. A form of catechesis that expounded the faith single-handedly, so to speak, directly from the Bible, without the apparent detour by way of dogma, could claim to be a catechetical method that was especially oriented to the sources. But when it was put into practice, something remarkable happened. The initial freshness of this new approach, which dealt directly with the Bible, did not last very long. Certainly, at first it really did bring much that was fruitful, beautiful, and enriching into religious instruction. You could smell the "fragrance of the Palestinian soil" and experience the human drama out of which and in which the Bible grew. But soon it became apparent that there was another side to this procedure, which J. A. Möhler described 150 years ago in a classic passage from his book *Unity in the Church*. He characterizes as follows the beauty, the immediacy, and the indispensable contribution of dealing directly with Scripture: "Without the Scriptures we would be deprived of the characteristic form of Jesus' discourses; we would not know how the God-man spoke, and I think that I would no longer want to live if I could no longer hear him speak." But Möhler goes on to explain also why the Scriptures cannot be separated from the living community, the only context within which they are "Scripture" in the first place: "Yet without tradition we would not know *who* is speaking there and *what* he was proclaiming, and our joy at what he said would also be gone!" [4]

From a completely different standpoint we can find in Albert Schweitzer's history of the research into the "historical Jesus" a description of what took place in the catechesis that was oriented exclusively to the literary source.

---

[4] J. A. Möhler, *Die Einheit in der Kirche*, ed. J. R. Geiselmann (Darmstadt, 1957), p. 54.

What became of the research into the historical Jesus is remarkable. It set out to find the Jesus of history, thinking that it could then situate [*hineinstellen*] him in our own time just as he is, as Teacher and Savior. It loosed the bonds with which he had been chained for centuries to the rocks of Church doctrine, and then it rejoiced when the figure again showed life and movement and it saw the historical Jesus coming toward it. He did not stop walking, however; instead he went right past our time and returned to his own.[5]

And in fact, this process, with which Schweitzer thought that he was marking the end of a phase in theology almost a century ago, has been repeated again and again in different variations in modern theology and in modern catechesis. For the documents—which scholars were now trying to read with no other mediation than that of the historical-critical method—retreated for that very reason into the distance of historical record. A form of exegesis in which the Bible no longer lives and is no longer understood as part of the living organism of the Church becomes necrophilia: the dead burying their dead.

This is manifested concretely first by the fact that the Bible thereby disintegrates as a Sacred Book and becomes a rather heterogeneous collection of literature. This gives rise to the question: Where does one want to settle in this literature, and by what criteria will one select the texts upon which to build? How quickly such developments can take place is evident, for instance, from the fact that in a recent letter to the editor of a German periodical the writer made the suggestion that in new editions of the Bible what is

---

[5] Quoted in W. G. Kümmel, *Das Neue Testament—Geschichte der Erforschung seiner Probleme* (Freiburg, 1958), p. 305.

dated [*das Zeitbedingte*] and outmoded should be printed in small type, and conversely what is valid should be emphasized accordingly. But what is valid? What is outmoded? In the end, such questions are decided as matters of taste, and what is left of the Bible then is just good enough to provide applause for what we ourselves want. But the Bible disintegrates in another way, too. In seeking the most ancient passages, which at the same time are regarded as the only sure and reliable material, we come upon the sources behind the sources, which ultimately become more important than the "source text" itself. And so a mother in Germany once told me that her son was becoming well acquainted in grade school with the Christology of Q [the supposed source of the sayings of Jesus], even though he had not yet heard a thing about the seven sacraments or the articles of the Creed. This means that, according to the criterion of the oldest stage of a given text as the most reliable historical testimony, the real Bible disappears behind the reconstructed Bible, behind the Bible as it supposedly ought to be. From this perspective, even the Jesus of the Gospels is already a Christ who has been repeatedly reshaped by dogma, and one must go back behind him to the Jesus of the *logia* source, or of other hypothetical sources, in order to get to the real Jesus. This "real" Jesus then no longer says and does anything that we do not like. He spares us, for example, the Cross as a sacrifice of atonement; the Cross is reduced to the status of a troublesome accident over which we should not linger too long. And the Resurrection becomes an experience of the disciples to the effect that Jesus (or at least his "cause") lives on. We encounter, no longer the events, but rather the consciousness of the disciples and of the "community" that has constructed them. The certainty of the faith is replaced by the self-assurance of the historical

hypothesis. Now this does indeed sound to me like an excit-
ing procedure. The self-assurance of the hypothesis, in not
a few catechetical presentations as well, plainly has a higher
status than the certainty of the faith, which seems to have
sunk to the level of an indefinite trust without clear content. But life is not a hypothesis; nor is death one, either;
and so we are left in the glass display case of the intellectual
world of things that we have made ourselves and can take
back again. But that is precisely why we are agitated by a
dismaying helplessness when faced with what is real—life
and death itself. Maybe it has to do with the fact that there
seems to be an increasingly insistent attempt to be able to
"make" man himself; if he were to become something man-
made, something that could be manufactured, then we would
finally be rid of the mystery of life. And could we then
perhaps "make" death, too, without pangs of conscience,
before it becomes a mystery that places mankind on the
edge of the mysterious abyss of nothingness and being?

But let us return to our topic. If we summarize our reflections thus far, we can ascertain, first of all, that the radical
change in catechesis in the last twenty or thirty years was
characterized by a new immediacy, by more direct access to
the written sources of the faith, to the Bible. Whereas previously the Bible entered into instruction in the faith only
in a manner mediated by the schema of Church teaching,
now there was an attempt to lead people to Christianity by
means of a direct dialogue between present-day experiences and the biblical message. What was gained by this
effort was an increase in humanity and concreteness in the
presentation of the foundations of Christian life. Dogma
was not denied for the most part in this development, but
it declined in importance to become a sort of external frame

of reference [*Orientierungsrahmen*] that no longer had much significance for the structure of catechesis or for its contents. Behind this was a certain embarrassment with regard to dogma, which stemmed from the unanswered question about the relation between the dogmatic and the historical-critical interpretation of Scripture. To the extent that this development progressed, it then became evident that Scripture, now left standing alone, was beginning to unravel. It was subjected over and over again to new "re-readings"; in the attempt to make the past present, personal experience obviously became the ultimate standard for what is relevant to the present [*gegenwartsfähig*]. The result is a sort of theological empiricism, in which the experience of the group, of the parish, or of the "experts" (= the manager of the experiences) becomes the supreme source. Thereby the common sources are then channeled in such a way that little of their original dynamic is still recognizable. Whereas traditional catechesis, in its day, had been accused of not leading us to the sources but rather of carefully filtering and bringing its water to the people through pipelines, now those former "pipelines" look like a pristine mountain stream in comparison with the new method of dealing with the sources. One thing has become amply clear: the question related to our topic, namely, the question of how the fresh water of the sources themselves can be preserved in handing on the faith, is more than ever the central question of catechesis today. With that, two of the main problems with our present situation are evident—problems that it is especially important to solve correctly:

a. The question of the relation between the dogmatic and the historical-critical interpretation of Scripture is urgent and must be tackled immediately. This is simultaneously the

question of how the living fabric of tradition and the rational methods of reconstructing the past can be set in relation to one another. Thus, however, it is also the question
about two levels of thinking and living: What position does
the rationality that is articulated in science properly assume
in the totality of human life and in its encounter with reality?

b. We noted a second problem in determining the relationship between method and content, of experience and
faith. It is clear that faith without experience necessarily
degenerates into an empty formulaic language. But it is plain
to see, conversely, that the reduction of faith to experience
would rob it of its core, since it intends, after all, to lead us
into the land of the not-yet-experienced and thus bring
us—as the psalm says—to that broad place where true life
begins to expand.

II. Toward Overcoming the Crisis

1. *What Is Faith?*

Of course, it would again be an unacceptable misapplica-
tion of academic procedure if we were to postpone the
renewal of catechesis until these questions had been "discussed thoroughly". Life cannot wait until theorizing is over
and done with; on the contrary, theory needs the head start
that life has, since it is always today's life. Faith itself is a form
of anticipation. It reaches ahead toward that which is actually still unreachable for us. Precisely in this way it brings the
unattainable into our life and carries our life beyond its own
limitations. To put it another way: for the correct theoretical
and practical solution to the crisis in handing on the faith, as
well as for a genuine renewal of catechesis, it is indispensable

that the aforementioned questions be acknowledged as questions and that we arrive at an answer to them. Yet this indispensability of theory, even in the Church and for the faith, does not mean that faith should be dissolved in theory or is completely dependent upon theory. Theological discussion is possible and meaningful at all when and because there is constantly a prior datum [*Vorgabe*] of reality. The First Letter of John speaks emphatically of this in a crisis situation quite similar to ours when its says: "But you have been anointed by the Holy One, and you all know" (1 Jn 2:20). This means: your baptismal faith, the knowledge communicated in the anointing (in the sacrament), is contact with reality itself and hence has priority over theory. The baptismal faith does not have to prove its credentials to theory, but rather theory must prove itself in the presence of reality, to the "knowledge" of the truth that is given in the baptismal profession of faith. A few verses farther on, the Apostle quite emphatically sets a limit to the intellectual claim that had set *gnosis*, that is, intellectual theory, above *pistis*, that is, above the Church's profession of faith. because what is at stake is the continued existence of Christianity or, alternatively, its reabsorption into the debate among the philosophers of that time. "The anointing which you received from him [= the knowledge of the faith within the Church's communion with the Spirit] abides in you, and you have no need that any one should teach you; as his anointing [= his Spirit, the Church's Spirit-given faith in Christ] teaches you about everything, and is true, and is no lie, just as it has taught you, abide in him" (1 Jn 2:27). Here, in the name of the apostolic authority of the disciple who had touched the Word-made-flesh, the faithful are challenged to resist the disintegration of their faith into theories, which are undertaken in the name of the authority of the intellect. This says to Christians that their authority, the "court of appeal"

of the Church's faith, pure and simple, is higher than the
authority of theological theory, because their faith expresses
the Church's life, which has a higher standing than theological explanations and the reliability of their hypotheses.[6]

With these references to the prerogatives of the baptismal faith over and against all didactic and theological theories, however, we already find ourselves in the midst of
answering the fundamental question of this presentation. In
order to elaborate these insights in greater depth, we must
now frame our question even more precisely. It concerns
the position of the sources of the faith in the transmission
of the faith. In order to answer correctly, we must therefore
clarify what is understood by faith and what a "source of
faith" actually is. The problem with the word "believe" lies
in the fact that it designates two completely different intellectual attitudes. In colloquial speech, to believe means the
same as "to think, suspect", that is, a preliminary degree of
knowledge with regard to things about which certainty is
not yet attainable. And so, indeed, there is a widespread
notion that the Christian faith, too, is a collection of con-
jectures about things that are not yet accessible to exact
science. Such an understanding misses the very essence of
belief. The most important Catholic catechism [as of 1983],
the *Roman Catechism* published during the reign of Pope
Pius V following the Council of Trent, comments on the
purpose and content of catechesis, noting that the sum total
of Christian knowledge is expressed in the saying of the
Redeemer that John has handed down: "This is eternal life,

[6] This is also the basic position of Saint Irenaeus in his controversy with
Gnosticism, which laid the foundations for Catholic theology in general and
had and still has decisive importance for both the formation and also the
continued existence of the Catholic Church. Cf. H. J. Jaschke, *Der Heilige
Geist im Bekenntnis der Kirche* (Münster, 1976), pp. 265–94.

that they know you the only true God, and Jesus Christ
whom you have sent" (Jn 17:3).[7] The *Catechism* means to
explain thereby the content and objective of all catechesis,
and in doing so it also explains fundamentally what faith is:
faith is aimed at being able to live. It involves not just any
ability, which someone can acquire or set aside; rather, it is
precisely a question of acquiring life itself, a life that is worth
living always and is capable of lasting forever. In the fourth
century Saint Hilary, in his book about God, described the
point of departure in his search for God in a very similar
way: he finally realized that life cannot be given merely for
the sake of dying. At the same time it became clear to him
that two vital goals, which first come to mind as the stuff
of life, fall short: neither property nor undisturbed security
in which to enjoy life is enough. "Things and security"
cannot constitute life, he says, because then man's only obligations would be to his belly and to his sloth.[8]

The summit of life is reached only at the place where
other things are found: knowledge and love. One could also
say that only relationship enriches life—the relationship of
"I" to "Thou", the relationship to the universe—yet even
these alone are still insufficient. "This is eternal life, that
they know *you* . . . ." Faith is life, because it is relationship;
a knowledge that becomes love and love that comes from
knowledge and leads to knowledge. Just as faith means
another sort of ability than the ability to accomplish particular tasks, namely, the very ability to live, so too it also
concerns another level of being and of knowing than the
knowledge of this or that particular thing: it has to do with
the very basic recognition in which we become aware of

---

[7] *Catechismus Romanus*, procemium X.
[8] Hilarius, *De trinitate* I, 1 and 2, C. Chr. LXII (Smulders edition), 1f.

our foundation, learn to accept it, and, because we have a foundation, are able to live. Hence the essential task of catechesis is to lead to the knowledge of God and of the One whom he has sent, or, as the *Roman Catechism* advisedly says: to remind people of this knowledge, for it is written in the deepest part of each and every one of us.

In the foregoing considerations we have traced what could be called the personalistic character of faith. But that is only half of the whole. A second aspect must be added to it, which we can again find presented in the First Letter of John. The very first verse describes the Apostle's experience as a seeing and touching of the Word that is life and that became tangible because it became flesh. From this resulted the Apostle's task of passing on what he had seen and heard, "so that you can enter together with us into this fellowship or 'communion' with the Word" (cf. 1 Jn 1:1–4). Faith, therefore, is not only directed frontally toward the "Thou" of God and Christ; this contact, rather, which is inaccessible for man by himself, is revealed in communion with those to whom he has communicated himself. This communion—we might add—is the gift of the Holy Spirit, who first builds for us the bridge to the Father and the Son. Faith, therefore, has not only an "I" and a "Thou", but also a "We"; in this "We" lives every memory that enables us to recover what has been forgotten: God and the One whom he has sent.

In other words, there is no faith without the Church. Henri de Lubac has shown that the "I" of the Christian professions of faith is not the isolated ego of the individual person; rather, it is the collective "I" of the Church.[9] When I say, "I believe", then this means precisely that I am going

[9] Henri de Lubac, *Geheimnis aus dem wir leben*, trans. Karlheinz Bergner and Hans Urs von Balthasar (Einsiedeln, 1967), p. 68.

beyond the limits of my private subjectivity so as to enter into the collective subject of the Church and, in her, to enter into the knowledge that transcends the ages and the limits of time. The act of faith is always an act of becoming a participant in a totality; it is an act of *communio*, a willingness to be incorporated into the communion of witnesses, so that we with them and in them may touch the untouchable, hear the inaudible, and see the invisible. Again, de Lubac has shown that we do not believe "in" the Church in the same way that we believe "in God". Instead, our faith is from the outset a believing together with the whole Church; only in this way is it epistemologically comprehensible and justifiable in the first place.[10] Therefore, whenever someone supposes that he can leave the faith of the Church out of catechesis to a greater or lesser extent, so as to experience it more immediately and accurately from Scripture directly, he is venturing into a zone of abstractions. For then one is no longer living and thinking and speaking out of a certainty that transcends the potential of the individual ego, the certainty of a larger memory that touches the very foundation and is touched by it; then one is no longer speaking with an authority that goes beyond the capability of every individual. Instead, one is dipping into that other sort of faith, which is a more or less well-founded opinion about unknown things. Then catechesis becomes one theory alongside others, one kind of knowledge among others; in this way it can no longer be the learning and receiving of life itself, that is, of eternal life.

[10] Henri de Lubac, *The Christian Faith: An Essay on the Structure of the Apostles' Creed*, trans. Richard Arnandez (San Francisco: Ignatius Press, 1986), pp. 317–53. Cf. Ratzinger, *Principles of Catholic Theology*, pp. 15–27. Especially important also are the clarifying remarks made by Louis Bouyer, *Le Métier du théologien* (Paris, 1979), pp. 207–27.

2. *What Are "Sources"?*

If we consider the faith from this perspective, then the question concerning the sources is also framed differently. About thirty years ago [in the 1950s], when I was trying to write a study on the ways that revelation was understood in thirteenth-century theology, I stumbled upon the unexpected fact that in that period it had not occurred to anyone to characterize the Bible as "revelation". Nor was the term "source" applied to it. This is not to say that the Bible was held in less esteem then than it is today. Quite the contrary: the respect for it was much more unconditional, and it was clear that theology, by right, can and should be nothing other than the interpretation of Scripture. But their concept of the harmony between what is written and what is lived out was different from contemporary notions. Therefore the term "revelation" was applied only, on the one hand, to that ineffable act which can never be adequately expressed in human words, in which God makes himself known to his creature, and, on the other hand, to that act of reception in which this gracious condescension [*Zuwendung*] of God dawns upon man and becomes revelation. Everything that can be grasped in words, and thus Scripture, too, is then testimony to that revelation but is not revelation itself. And only revelation itself is also a "source" in the strict sense, the source by which Scripture is nourished. If it becomes disengaged from this living connection to God's condescension within the "We" of the faithful, then it is uprooted from the ground in which it lives and becomes merely "the letter", merely "the flesh".[11] Much,

[11] Due to various circumstances, until now I have been able to publish only fragments of my research from that time. See "Offenbarung—Schrift—Überlieferung", TThZ 67 (1958): 13–27; "Wesen und Weisen der *auctoritas*

much later, after the term "source" had acquired a histor-icist sense and had then been applied to the Bible, the intrin-sic and essential self-transcendence of Scripture was thereby excluded at the same time, and so reading the Bible nec-essarily became one-dimensional as well. It could now arrive only at what is historically probable, but the fact that God acts is just not part of what a historian could or should regard as probable.

When one views the Bible merely as a source in the sense in which that is understood by the historical-critical method (which it no doubt *also* is), then the only competence that there can be in interpreting it is that of the historian. It also follows that only historical questions can be investi-gated on the basis of this "source". The historian, however, has to try, if at all possible, to turn a God who acts in his-tory into an unnecessary hypothesis. If, on the other hand, the Bible is the precipitate (or product) of a much greater, perpetually inexhaustible process of revelation, and if accord-ingly its contents only come to the reader's attention when this greater event has touched him, then this does not dimin-ish the Bible's importance, but it does fundamentally trans-form the question about competency in interpreting it. For that means that the Bible is part of a referential context, in which the living God communicates himself in Christ through the Holy Spirit. It means that it is the expression and instrument of that communion, in which the "I" of God and the "Thou" of man come into contact within the

---

im Werk des hl. Bonaventura", in: *Die Kirche und ihre Ämter und Stände*, commemorative volume for Cardinal Frings (Cologne, 1960), pp. 58–72; and also several references in my book *Die Geschichtstheologie des hl. Bonaventura* (Munich, 1959). See also on this difficulty: Henri de Lubac, *Exégèse médiévale*, 4 vols. (Paris, 1959–1964).

.

"We" of the Church that Christ has inaugurated. [The Bible] is then part of a living organism, through which it came into being in the first place—an organism that through the vicissitudes of history has nevertheless maintained its identity and hence holds the "copyright" to the Bible, as it were, and can speak about it as its very own. The fact that the Bible—like any work of art and even more than all other works of art—says far more than what can be demonstrably gathered from the letters of the text in a given reading follows from the fact that it puts into language, after all, a revelation that is reflected in the words without being exhaustively expressed in them. This also explains why, when revelation has "arrived" and has again become a living revelation, the result is a deeper union with the Word than when it is merely analyzed as a text. Hence it follows quite logically that the "sympathy" of the saints with the Bible, their compassion with the Word, was able to understand more of it than all the methods and devices of the Enlightenment. In this way the phenomenon of tradition also becomes comprehensible as well as the phenomenon of the Church's Magisterium.[12]

What does this mean for our topic? If the foregoing description is correct, then in catechesis the historical sources necessarily have to be viewed at all times in connection with the real source, namely, with the God who acts in

[12] The Bible itself presupposes these connections and accordingly is read from its own perspective only when the reader approaches it in this way; this is convincingly demonstrated with linguistic methods by P. G. Müller, *Der Traditionsprozeß im Neuen Testament* (Freiburg, 1981). Important points of view are offered by H. Gese, *Zur biblischen Theologie* (Munich, 1977), pp. 9–30. On the Church's nature as a subject, see the document issued by the International Theological Commission, *Die Einheit des Glaubens und der theologische Pluralismus* (Einsiedeln, 1973), especially my commentary on Theses IV–VII, pp. 32–48.

Christ. This source, however, can be accessed only within that living organism which created it and continually keeps it alive. In this organism the books of Sacred Scripture and the declarations of the Church's faith that explain them are not dead witnesses of past things; rather, they are the sustaining elements of a common life. Here they have never ceased being a present reality while at the same time delimiting the present; inasmuch as they bring us together with the One who holds time in his hands, they also make the boundaries between the ages permeable. The past and the future touch one another in the today of the faith.[13]

3. *The Structure of Catechesis*

a. The four principal divisions

This intrinsic connection between the Word and the organism that conveys it also marks out the way for catechesis. Its framework follows from the fundamental events in the life of the Church, which correspond to the essential dimensions of Christian life. Thus in the earliest period a catechetical structure developed that at its core goes back to the origins of the Church, a structure as old as or even older than the canon of biblical writings. Luther used this structure for his catechism, taking it for granted just as the authors of the *Roman Catechism* did. This was possible because it was a question, not of an artificial system, but of a simple arrangement of the requisite memorized material of the faith,

---

[13] That is why the liturgical "Hodie" [today], like the "Cras videbitis" [tomorrow you will see], from the vigils of Christmas and Easter respectively, are not frivolous wordplay, but rather enunciate a reality within the context of the faith.

which at the same time mirrors the elements of the Church's life: the Apostles' Creed, the sacraments, the Ten Commandments and the Lord's Prayer. These four classical "principal divisions" of catechesis have sufficed over the centuries as organizational subdivisions and collecting points for catechetical instruction and have simultaneously opened the way into the Bible as well as into the living Church. We have just said that that they correspond to the dimensions of Christian life; the *Roman Catechism* spells this out when it says that it presents what the Christian must believe (Creed), what he must hope (Our Father), and what he must do (the Ten Commandments as an interpretation of the greatest Commandment and that it also defines the environment in which all of this is anchored (sacrament and Church).[14]

Another immediate result of this is a harmony with the four levels of exegesis of which the Middle Ages spoke and which it regarded furthermore as corresponding to the levels of human existence. First there is the literal sense, that is, attention to the historical ground of the biblical events. Then comes the so-called allegorical sense, that is, an examination of the inner transcendence of these events, by dint of which the history described in these pages can be characterized as salvation history. Then, finally, there are the moral and the anagogical senses, which show how action follows from being and how history is not merely happening but, beyond that, hope, a sacrament of what is yet to come.[15] This doctrine concerning the four senses of Scripture ought to be studied again today. It indicates the irreplaceable locus of strictly historical exegesis but also clearly notes its limits and its necessary context. Hence in this collection

---

[14] *Catechismus Romanus*, procemium XII.
[15] Cf. Henri de Lubac, *Der geistige Sinn der Schrift* (Einsiedeln, 1952).

of requisite memorized material of the faith that is presented by the four "principal divisions", there is an internal logic, to be sure. The *Roman Catechism* therefore advisedly describes them also as the *loci* or centers of activity for interpreting the Bible. In contemporary scientific language one might say that the *Catechism* means for them to be understood as successive points in a thematic organization and hermeneutic of Scripture.[16]

It is inexplicable why some people today think that this simple, theologically and pedagogically correct structure has to be abandoned at all costs. In the initial phases of the new catechetical movement it was considered too simpleminded. Experts were absolutely convinced that they had to construct rigorously logical and systematic presentations of the Christian message. Such attempts at systematization have their place in theological reflection, but they do not belong in catechesis; they seldom survive their authors. The opposite extreme, the loss of all structure and random

---

[16] *Catechismus Romanus*, prooemium XII speaks of "quattuor his quasi communibus sacrae theologiae locis" [four . . . general heads of Sacred Scripture]; XIII mentions "prima illa quattuor genera" [the four heads already enumerated]; the word "source" comes into play earlier in XIII, when it says that every statement in the Bible can be traced back to one of these *loci*, to which the catechist should have recourse as the source of the particular doctrine he is explaining ("quo tanquam ad eius doctrinae fontem . . . confugiens"). This observation seems to me to be significant, both for the use of the word "source" and for the objective understanding of the factors involved in Christian instruction. Here the Bible is not regarded as the source in contrast to the *capita* as an organizational schema, but rather the *capita* are the source from which the partial statements of the Bible flow. This is true of the Decalogue in its relation to the Old Testament books of the Law, as H. Gese has impressively made clear using the methods of modern exegesis in his groundbreaking discussion of the Law: H. Gese, *Zur biblischen Theologie* (Munich, 1977), pp. 55–84. This could be shown, not quite in the same way but in an analogous manner, for the other *capita* as well.

selection determined by contemporary situations, almost inevitably follows such exaggerated forms of systematic thinking.

b. Remarks on two problems of content

It is not within the scope of this lecture to go into the contents of the four principal divisions of catechesis; our task here is to deal only with the questions of structure. Nevertheless I cannot refrain from adding a few brief remarks about two aspects of this structure that are particularly at risk today. The first point concerns the place assigned to the belief in God the Creator and in his creation within the Church's profession of faith. Again and again one hears misgivings, as though too strong an emphasis on this aspect of the faith could endanger the central importance of Christology.[17] There may well be reasons for such misgivings, in light of earlier stages of theological development. But today it seems to me that the opposite concern is much more appropriate: the marginalization of the doctrine of creation is having a reductive effect on the concept of God and, therefore, on Christology as well. Anything having to do with religion is classified nowadays as psychology or sociology; the material world is relegated to the departments of physics and engineering. Yet only if being itself, including matter, comes from God's hands and remains in God's hands can God really be our savior and grant us life—real life. Today there is a fatal tendency, wherever matter comes into play in the beliefs that we proclaim, to balk and retreat into the symbolic; this happens starting with creation, through

[17] This fear is voiced also in Conférence épiscopale française, *La Catéchèse des enfants*, p. 37, although we have to agree entirely with the main thesis, that the doctrine of creation, too, should be examined from a christological perspective.

the Virgin Birth of Jesus and his Resurrection, to the Real
Presence of Christ in the transubstantiation of bread and
wine, and on to our resurrection and the Lord's Second
Coming. It is hardly an indifferent theological debate when
the resurrection of the individual is relocated in death, which
is not only to deny the soul, but also to dispute the genuine corporeality of salvation.[18] A decisive renewal of faith
in creation is thus the prerequisite also for the credibility
and depth of Christology and eschatology.

The second point that I would like to emphasize concerns
the Ten Commandments. On the basis of a fundamental mis-
understanding of the Pauline critique of the Law, many are
of the opinion that the Decalogue, being "the Law", has to
be eliminated from catechesis and replaced, preferably by the
Beatitudes from the Sermon on the Mount. But that is to misunderstand both the Decalogue and the Sermon on the Mount
and, hence, the entire structure of the Bible. Paul, on the contrary, described the New Testament revolution with regard
to the position of the Law with the formula "fulfillment of
the law through love", and in elucidating this he referred
explicitly to the tradition of the Ten Commandments (see Rom
13:8–10; cf. Lev 19:18; Ex 20:13ff. and Deut 5:17ff.).[19] When
the Ten Commandments are taken out of catechesis, this affects
its fundamental structure, and then it does not really accomplish its task of introducing the catechumens into the faith of
the Church.[20]

---

[18] Concerning this set of questions, see: J. Ratzinger, *Eschatologie* (Regens-
burg, 1977), as well as the more complete and in-depth statements in my
article "Zwischen Tod und Auferstehung", *Internationale katholische Zeitschrift*
9 (1980): 209–23.

[19] Cf. Gese, *Zur biblischen Theologie*, especially p. 55.

[20] The reference text, Conférence épiscopale française, *La Catéchèse des
enfants*, is to be credited with clearly highlighting the lasting validity of the

c. On the formal structure of catechesis

I would like to conclude these reflections with two supplementary comments on the theological questions mentioned in the first part of our discussion. The first comment concerns the question of the relation between the dogmatic and the historical interpretation of Scripture. At the origins of that turn toward a direct involvement with Scripture, which simultaneously introduced a turn away from catechetical and dogmatic tradition, was the fear that the subordination to dogma would not allow for a truly free and comprehensive reading of the Bible. In practice, the handling of dogmatic tradition in interpreting Scripture provided very real grounds for those fears. We see today, however, that only the context of the Church's tradition allows us to adhere to the whole Bible and the real Bible. Today we see that only within the context of the communal faith of the Church is it possible to take the Bible at its word and to believe what is said in it as reality, as a factual account about this world of ours and as history. This provides, then, a historical justification as well for the dogmatic interpretation of Scripture: The hermeneutic locus "Church" is the only one that can adhere to the writings of the Bible as Scripture and accept what they themselves say as meaningful and true. All this notwithstanding, there will always be a certain tension between the ever-new questions of history and the continuity of the faith. At the same time, however, it has by now become quite clear that traditional faith

---

Ten Commandments (p. 59). In addition, the mention of the sacramental character of catechesis (pp. 57f.) is congruent with our purpose in this presentation.

is not the enemy but rather the guarantor of historical fidelity [*Treue*] with regard to the Bible.

My second and final remark returns again to the question of method and content. It may surprise today's reader to learn that the *Roman Catechism* in the sixteenth century was fully aware of the problem of catechetical methodology. It remarks that a lot depends on whether the instructor teaches something in one way or another. Therefore one must carefully study the age, intellectual ability, way of life, and social situation of the listeners, so as really to become all things to all men. The catechist must know who needs milk and who eats solid food, and he should adapt his teaching to the ability of the listeners to absorb it. The biggest surprise for us, however, may be the fact that this catechism allows the catechist much more freedom than contemporary catechetics, generally speaking, is inclined to do. Indeed, it leaves it to the instructor to determine the sequence of topics in his catechesis, depending on the persons being instructed and time constraints—assuming, of course, that the catechist himself is personally dedicated and lives a life based on an ongoing meditation upon his material and that he keeps in view the four principal divisions of catechesis and coordinates his own plan with them.[21] The *Roman Catechism* deliberately does not claim to specify any particular didactic arrangement; instead, it says: "Whatever plan the catechist chooses, we have decided in this book to follow the approach taken by the Church Fathers."[22] In other words,

---

[21] *Catechism of the Council of Trent*, trans. and notes by John A. McHugh, O.P., and Charles J. Callan, O.P. (New York: Wagner, 1943), preface, question 13, pp. 10–11: "*Docendi autem ordinem eum adhibebit, qui et personis et tempori accommodatus videbitur.*" The other citations are from question 12 of the preface.

[22] Ibid., preface XIII.

this means that it makes available to the catechist the indispensable basic divisions of catechesis and their particular
contents, but it does not relieve him of the responsibility to
seek the appropriate way of communicating them in a given
situation. No doubt the *Roman Catechism* presupposed a second level of literature to help the catechist in this endeavor,
without itself trying to program in advance every particular
situation.

I consider this distinction among various levels to be
extremely important. There are many reasons for the mis-
erable state of recent catechesis, not the least of which is
the fact that instructors have obviously forgotten the difference between "text" and "commentary". The text, that
is to say, the actual content of what has to be said, progres-
sively disappeared in the commentary, but in that way the
commentary no longer had anything to comment on. It
became its own standard and thus lost its seriousness. I am
of the opinion that the *Roman Catechism*'s distinction between
the basic text of the proclamation of the faith and the spoken or written texts by which it is imparted is by no means
just one didactic path among other possible methods; rather,
it is an essential part of the matter.[23] This distinction, on
the one hand, fosters the necessary freedom of the catechist
in responding to various situations; on the other hand, it is
indispensable if the identity of the faith-content is to be
ensured. Nor can anyone object that all human speech about

---

[23] This orderly gradation is already clear in the second century in the
interrelated arrangement: Creed—*regula fidei* [rule of faith]—catechetical treatises. Whereas the Creed offers the universal terminology of the prayerful
profession of the faith, the *regula*, which does not consist of set formulas, is
still a basic arrangement, presented to the individual instructor, of the *capita*
of Christianity, an arrangement that is then in turn reflected and applied
concretely to various situations in the theological literature.

the faith is already commentary and no longer the "original text", because we can never capture God's Word perfectly in human words. The fact that God's Word is indeed always infinitely greater than any human word, even greater than the inspired human words of Scripture, does not mean, nevertheless, that the message of the faith has no contours and no face. Rather, this compels us all the more to preserve what precedes and is presented to our thinking—namely, the common faith of the Church, nourished by Scripture—as our common ground. We will have to attempt to explain this ground anew in ever-changing situations, so as to correspond through the ages to the inexhaustibility of revelation. I believe that it is therefore necessary to distinguish clearly again the levels of the catechetical testimony [*Aussage*] in their printed forms as well, that is, to venture to teach catechism as a Catechism, so that then the commentary can be commentary and the proper relation between sources and intermediate texts can be restored.

I can think of no better conclusion for these reflections than the words with which the oft-cited *Roman Catechism* describes the goal of catechesis: "The whole purpose of teaching and instruction must be directed toward the love that never ceases. For whatever is proposed by the pastor, whether it be the exercise of faith, of hope, or of some moral virtue, the love of the Lord should at the same time be so strongly insisted upon as to show clearly that all the works of perfect Christian virtue can have no other origin, no other end than divine love." [24]

---

[24] *Catechism of the Council of Trent*, preface X, p. 7.

Reflection by Pierre Eyt

Rector of the Institut Catholique de Paris

Although its immediate subject was *catechesis*, the conference given by Cardinal Joseph Ratzinger appeared to many of us to go far beyond this question so as to elaborate on the theology of the Word of God, of the Church, and of the faith. Some may have been surprised to find that, with reference to *catechesis*, a comprehensive overview of the phenomenon of Christianity was presented to us. This may be because to some extent we had lost sight of the specifically theological situation and function of *catechesis* to risk favoring a form of *religious instruction* that was derived one-sidedly here or there from experimental teaching methods.

Those who have read works by Cardinal Ratzinger find again in his conference the major issues and strength of conviction of a genuine theologian, even though the parameters of a conference necessarily diminish their dynamic persuasiveness and, at the same time, also blur some of the nuances.

Joseph Ratzinger is well acquainted with the Fathers of the Church. He readily takes up his position in the footsteps of his master, Saint Augustine. It is from the latter, it seems to me, that he adopts the perspective that constitutes the axis around which his reflections have revolved for the past three decades upon the Mystery of the Church, or, more precisely, on the simultaneously maternal and fraternal Mystery of the Church.

41

By the Church, [he tells us] we understand, on the one
hand, an "institution" that precedes the individual and, on
the other hand, a community made up of individuals. She
is, in the first case, the sum total of the means of arriving at
communion with God and, in the second case, a community that is created thereby. Or to put it still another way,
the Church can be understood, from one perspective, as
the actualization of Christ's saving power and, thus, the institution that precedes the life of the individual and, as a structure, presents the face of the whole—yet also, from another
perspective, participation in the life of Christ, communion
of life with him, and, thus, that which is ordered to the
structure and without which the structure would be nothing but an empty framework.[1]

The approach and perspective of Joseph Ratzinger open up
for us a path to a *theology* of the Church. This is worth
focusing our attention on first.

I. The Church and Catechesis

Ratzinger's firmly held belief is based on the priority of
the Church with respect to Scripture. Why does he make
that remark? No doubt in doing so the theologian is only
repeating an assertion of the Church Fathers, for example,
of Saint Irenaeus of Lyons: "If the apostles themselves had
not left us any Scripture, would we not have to follow
the order of the tradition they handed down to those to
whom they entrusted the Churches?" (*Adversus haereses*,
III, 4, 5). For Joseph Ratzinger, as for the Fathers, the

---

[1] Joseph Ratzinger, *Das neue Volk Gottes: Entwürfe zur Ekklesiologie* (Düs-
seldorf: Patmos, 1969), pp. 242 ff. [Translated from the German text as para-
phrased by Hans Urs von Balthasar in: *Die Krise der Katechese und ihre
Überwindung* (Einsiedeln: Johannes Verlag, 1983), pp. 40–41.—TRANS.]

expression "tradition of the Church" means that Jesus' message and its contents come down to us through a unique and living community, which has remained the same since the first witnesses, the apostles. This community is united by the same faith that, from the beginning, has been nourished by the same apostolic source. And so Irenaeus of Lyons can write about his master Polycarp "that he taught only what he learned from the apostles, what the Church has handed down, which alone is true" (*Adversus haereses*, III, 3, 4). The Incarnation of the Word in Jesus Christ inaugurated the time and opened up the place of the salvific mission: the *Son*, sent by the *Father*; the *Spirit*, sent by the Father and the Son; the *Church*, sent by the Son and the Spirit. "As the Father has sent me, even so I send you.... Receive the Holy Spirit" (Jn 20:21–22).

For the sake of the mission to which he assigned her, God entrusted to his Church the loving plan that he devised from all eternity for sinful man and for the world. The Word of God—the revelation of the Divine Mystery and the truth of salvation—is the source of all life. As such it was entrusted to the Church. The apostles who were witnesses of the risen Christ have handed on to the Church for all subsequent ages the revelation that they received from the Savior. Through intermediaries—both individuals and communities—and by the inspiration of the Holy Spirit, the Church would commit to writing a crucial part of the message transmitted to the apostles. These are the Gospels and the other New Testament writings. This Scripture, in its origin and in its content, is inseparable from the Church. Nor can it be dissociated from her if it is to be read, interpreted, and comprehended. Therefore Scripture has its origin and takes its place within a broader context and milieu. Thus it cannot be separated from the

acts of the Church to which it bears witness, particularly
baptism and the Eucharist. Baptism and Eucharist occupy
the center of gravity of the Church. Scripture acquires its
authentic meaning only with reference to them.

Within this living organism it is imperative to refer to
the apostles, the first witnesses of the risen Lord, the first
envoys of the Spirit, the first links in Church tradition. It is
through them and in faithfulness that Jesus makes himself
known and offers mankind *the way* of divine salvation. And
so all the acts of the Church bear the mark of *apostolicity*:
Scripture and its interpretation, baptism, the Eucharist, the
ordination of ministers, the proclamation of the faith. . . .
All these essential elements in the life of Christian communities are interrelated with perfect reciprocity.

Now there is no disputing the fact that *catechesis* origi-
nally appears at this precise place. As the accompaniment
to the process of initiation to the faith, *catechesis* is nourished by Scripture and by the baptismal and eucharistic rites
for which it is a preparation. Therefore it expresses, in a
suitably adapted and progressive manner, the entire tradition of the Church. Inasmuch as it is involved in the liturgy, therefore, catechesis is not "just any instruction on a
religious subject, but a living, praying initiation that simultaneously takes as its point of departure the realities of worship, of the rites themselves, in order to explain them, and
aims to introduce the faithful into the mystery of the worship".[2] Catechesis, therefore, is not primarily related to the
universal human effort to instruct and educate, as though it
were the consistent application of that undertaking to the
Christian faith. More radically, the catechesis of the early
Church is based on the structure of communion with the

---

[2] A. G. Martimort, *L'Église en prière* (Paris: Desclée, 1951), p. 239.

Divine Mystery, which is accessible only in faith. That is why this catechesis is immediately related to the two fundamental acts of the Church, which are baptism and the Eucharist. Baptism, by its structure and by the role played in it by the Creed (*traditio* and *redditio symboli*), thus becomes the endpoint where initiation and catechesis come together. Therefore the purpose of catechesis as well as its basic mode of expression are best measured by taking the Church and the sacraments as one's point of departure: it is a question of introducing someone into the knowledge and then into a deeper understanding of the mystery of God and his love for mankind. Therefore there must be reference to the revelation of this mystery.

Revelation is the act of love by which God opens a way to himself and opens himself. Therefore it constitutes the staggering discovery brought about by faith. As a meeting with God through Christ, it is of course a personal encounter—the most personal encounter there is. Each person experiences it as engaging him entirely and as engaging what is most intimate, most individual, and most exclusive in him. The "I" feels that it is called, enveloped, and loved by a "Thou". Pope John Paul II, in his encyclical *Redemptor hominis*, has emphasized the highly personalized character of man according to Christ. Furthermore, is it not the act of faith in which he engages that best reveals to man his singular reality? "Unique and unrepeatable. . . . Man has a personal history of his life and above all a personal history of his soul." Now this history of each person culminates in the discovery of his created existence, which is maintained and directed by God's love.

In this discovery, I am not limited to *comprehending*, but rather I recognize that I myself am grasped and *comprehended* by one greater than I.[3] Such is the Mystery that precedes me and surpasses me and that I will never be able to overtake or exhaust completely. In any case, however great the disproportion may be with me personally, I perceive in this Mystery an orientation capable of limitless deepening and of a loving response that is as generous as possible.

We would be mistaken, however, if we thought that this revelation takes place in the sanctuary of an isolated consciousness. In fact, the ecclesial community already envelops us with its presence and its action at the very moment when God is discovered, however personal that discovery may be. Parents, friends, catechists, witnesses, books, the whole community, the gospel itself—all these intermediaries are the Church in her various forms of active presence. The "I" and the "Thou" of faith and of the encounter with God can commune only in the "We" of the Church, that is to say, within the community of those who share the same faith.[4] The discovery of God, of the covenant and of love in Christ will go hand in hand, then, with listening to the proclamation of the Word, deepening one's sacramental life, and serving one's neighbors in charity. Christian life consists of the *interweaving* of I and Thou, of I and We. Few theologians and spiritual writers have expressed this as insistently as Ratzinger.

This allows us to underscore how much the ecclesial community is present from the moment when faith is engendered—that faith that the community can best convey and nourish. Consequently catechesis is essentially different from any other type of pedagogy or process of

---

[3] Cf. J. Ratzinger, *Introduction to Christianity*, rev. ed. (San Francisco: Ignatius Press, 2004), p. 78.

[4] Ibid., p. 90.

acquiring knowledge. Catechesis does not consist in the first place of an encounter of the instructor's subjectivity with that of the students in the attempt to convey a conceptual content or a skill. It is instead a specific act of the Church introducing her children to a sacramental knowledge of the Truth that is Christ. That is why catechesis cannot be carried out apart from the sacraments of the Church, within an undifferentiated pedagogical framework designed merely for the exchange of information. On the contrary, catechesis is vitally dependent upon its intrinsic, direct, and immediate relationship to the sacraments of the faith, especially to baptism and the Eucharist.

Among the Fathers of the early Church, all of whom left some record of their catechetical experience, catechesis was nourished by the sacraments, by the sacramental rites, and by the texts that accompanied them. Furthermore it prepared for the conversion that these sacraments presupposed. Father Congar forcefully reminds us of this:

> The ancient patristic and liturgical texts express, with a richness that defies analysis, a continuity, indeed, a thoroughgoing unity in the faith that is conceived in the heart, progressively educated in the maternal bosom of the Church, professed in baptism, where man commits and consecrates himself, sanctioned by the physical act of baptism, and finally acknowledged before men and professed as praise in God's service.... When a believer followed this ascending path leading him into Christian life and introducing him into the life of the Church ... the apostolic faith was handed on, which is the very basis of tradition. It was handed on as a reality by all of these factors together: the Word of instruction, the practical discipline, the following of good example, entrance into a community with observable rules of

behavior, and the real and efficacious celebration of the sacrament. Yes, indeed, the result was the communication of
the reality and the totality of Christianity.[5]

II. Catechesis and the Creed

Since catechesis, via baptism and the Eucharist, is thus bound
up with the fundamental structure of the Church's life, it
cannot help but obey a certain number of rules that are,
strictly speaking, ecclesial. They are essentially derived from
baptism, understood as a sacrament of faith. But when we
say "are derived", we are not thinking of some abstract or
programmatic relationship, imagined from outside and a pri-
ori. We simply mean to say that the Fathers of the Church
structured their catechetical activity with a view to baptism
and taking it as their point of departure, since it was a matter of preparing the catechumens who requested the sacrament. But from this factual and historical given follows
organically a permanent constitutive law of catechesis: its
relation to baptism, whether not yet conferred on the
catechumen or already administered to the new Christian.
In this context it is legitimate to emphasize the twofold
importance of the *symbol* or creed, as witness to the tradition and as a *mnemonic* summary of the Church's faith. I
will dwell more on the first aspect because it allows us to
highlight the Cardinal's remarks on the place of Scripture
and the problem of *sources*.

From the very beginning the structure of baptism manifests its explicit connection with the faith. For Saint Mark
as well as Saint Matthew, faith is closely bound up with
the baptismal washing (Mt 28:19–20; Mk 16:15–16). The

[5] Yves Congar, *La Tradition et la vie de l'Église* (Paris: Fayard, 1963), p. 29.

connection between faith and baptism is attested by Saint Paul (Gal 3:26–27) and emphasized even more by the Acts of the Apostles (2:38–41; 8:12–13; 10:48; 16:14–15, and so on). This close connection would continue to develop and deepen, for example in the early Church of Rome or Milan.

> In describing the baptismal ritual, Hippolytus of Rome and Saint Ambrose, too, provide us with the text of the profession of faith and show how closely connected it was to the washing in water. The one who was baptizing descended into the pool with the candidate and then questioned him in succession about his faith in the Father, the Son, and the Holy Spirit. To each of these questions the candidate responded, *Credo*. After each response the minister placed his hand on the candidate's head and forced him to immerse himself completely in the water.[6]

With regard to baptism, then, catechesis sets forth the faith that will be *professed* at the baptism as well as the moral conduct of a Christian. The preparation for baptism very quickly acquired a highly organized structure. During one of the days devoted to it, this preparation included a remarkable act: the bishop *handed over* to the catechumen the text of the baptismal creed and explained it phrase by phrase. Eight days later, the catechumen *returned* the creed to the bishop by reciting it for him by heart. In both the East and the West, the liturgical action of the *traditio* and the *redditio symboli* demonstrates the organic connection between faith and baptism.[7] In Rome, the text that was *handed over* and *returned* in this way was the Apostles' Creed, which, as everyone knows, is made up of three parts, the first devoted to the Father, the second to the Son, and the third to the

[6] R. Beraudy, in Martimort, *Église en prière*, pp. 517–19.
[7] Cf. Congar, *Tradition et la vie de l'Église*, p. 29.

Holy Spirit. Starting from this initial text, other formulations would develop, but always following a similar pattern. At the very heart of the sacrament, the Creed introduces the presence of an ecclesial text that is considered to be *the faithful echo of the faith of the early Church and the faithful presentation of the core of the good news*. The faith is handed on, therefore, and this occurs at the solemn moment of baptism through the medium of a text elaborated by the Church. Emphasizing this fact leads us to note briefly several consequences, which Cardinal Ratzinger himself mentioned. First of all, the importance of the Creed as the heart of catechesis. We understand this even better now that we have seen its central role in the sacramental rite. This role cannot be explained solely in terms of mnemonic purposes, although these may also have been involved. The importance of the Creed, rather, is connected with what we have said about the Church and about the transmission of the faith effected by the community.

III. The Gospel as the Source of the Faith

The preeminent role of the Creed in Baptism and catechesis brings us now to another problem: that of the relationship between the Creed, doctrinal formulas, and the biblical writings. Would it not suffice, for example, to know the Gospel accounts and the Old Testament? Will not the Creed and the other formulations of the Church bar the way to that knowledge? I think that everyone will agree that we would not even be asking this question if it were not for the beneficial effects of the biblical renewal. The vital significance of this renewal for the Church must not be underestimated. In any case, here again, the previous works of Joseph Ratzinger and other theologians enable us to appreciate better the perspective that he proposes to us concerning recourse to Scripture and everything having to do with the notion of *source*.

Historians have discovered that the symbols of faith, like the *Apostles' Creed* or the *Niceno-Constantinopolitan Creed*, serve several purposes. Their liturgical function is to provide the text for a sort of hymn of faith to the Father, the Son, and the Spirit, and this is the role of the chanting of the *Credo* during the celebration of Mass on Sundays and feast days. We have already emphasized that the Apostles' *Creed* also serves as an instrument of baptismal catechesis or of elementary Christian instruction. The Apostles' Creed or the Nicene Creed can also provide a firm foundation for preaching and signposts or orientations for theology. But above all, because they enable and promote the profession of a common faith within the Church, the creeds also have a decisive importance, even in our days, in ecumenical dialogue. As for later doctrinal formulas, they most often had a noticeably different purpose, especially that of protecting the purity of doctrine and of instruction in the faith against interpretations that did not respect it completely.

Creeds and doctrinal formulas arising from tradition and ratified by the Magisterium of the popes, councils, or universal episcopate have a relationship of organic unity with Sacred Scripture that the Second Vatican Council clearly described in the Dogmatic Constitution on Divine Revelation. "In the supremely wise arrangement of God, sacred Tradition, sacred Scripture and the Magisterium of the Church are so connected and associated that one of them cannot stand without the others. Working together, each in its own way under the action of the Holy Spirit, they all contribute effectively to the salvation of souls" (*Dei Verbum*, no. 10). Given the bond of solidarity that unites tradition,

Scripture, and the Magisterium, it should be clear that we cannot pit one of these against the others but must always attempt to interpret each one in terms of the others. That is why each of them constitutes an authority for interpreting the others, and the Council has specified the rules for this process:

> The task of giving an authentic interpretation of the Word of God, whether in its written form or in the form of Tradition, has been entrusted to the living teaching office of the Church alone. Its authority in this matter is exercised in the name of Jesus Christ. Yet this Magisterium is not superior to the Word of God, but is its servant. It teaches only what has been handed on to it. At the divine command and with the help of the Holy Spirit, it listens to this devotedly, guards it with dedication and expounds it faithfully. All that it proposes for belief as being divinely revealed is drawn from this single deposit of faith. (*Dei Verbum*, no. 10)

Thus the Magisterium has the competence and the responsibility to interpret in an authentic manner the Word of God as it has been *written* or *handed down*. But at the same time the written Word of God, or Scripture (to confine ourselves here to that), constitutes an indispensable authority for reviewing statements by the Magisterium. This authority, however, cannot be viewed as standing in opposition to the Church or the Magisterium. As early as 1961, Ratzinger wrote that, as Catholic theology understands it, "the Word lives in the Church just as the Church lives on the Word, in a relationship of interdependence." This relationship of interdependence between the Word and the Church necessarily excludes both a subordination of the Church to a Word that would be independent of her and also the reverse, that is, a subordination of the Word to a

Church that would be all-powerful and manipulative in this regard. In his book *Das neue Volk Gottes* [The new people of God], Joseph Ratzinger notes, following a discussion of Luther's theology, that

> the connection between witness and Word is a reciprocal relationship. Not only is the Word bound up with the witness, but the witness is a witness only insofar as he for his part acknowledges that he is bound by the Word. Luther's protest probably would not have occurred in the first place had the second side of this relationship been realized as clearly and unambiguously as the first. In truth, we must admit that until now everything has been done to safeguard by all means the first side of the connection—the bond of the Word to the witness—but that there has been nowhere near as much concrete concern about guaranteeing the second side of the relationship—the bond of the witness in turn to the Word. And yet this would seem to be a crucial task, if the Catholic concept of the Church is to be credible in fact (and not just in theory): to clarify and emphasize again the authoritative and decisive character [*den Instanzcharakter*] of the Word itself, and not merely that of the witness, that is, of the ordained ministry. For there can be no doubt that the tendency to isolate the Word's bond to the witness and to make that bond autonomous, while ignoring the simultaneous bond of the witness to the Word, would be no less of a heresy than declaring the Word autonomous, which was (almost necessarily) the historical reaction against the preponderance of the ordained ministry over the Word in the late medieval Church.[8]

From this we can conclude that it is indispensable that Scripture should play a leading role in catechesis and that all the other statements about faith and charitable action must

---

[8] Ratzinger, *Neue Volk Gottes*, pp. 118–19 [translated from German].

continually be referred to Scripture in order to justify and explain them and to make them effective. An authentic catechesis, however, cannot present the contents of Scripture without situating them within the perspective of tradition and the Magisterium. In any case, the presentation of Scripture cannot explicitly or implicitly serve as a recourse or a sort of appeal to an "original" state of the faith that consequently possesses an authority superior or opposed to the Creed and the doctrinal formulas. Such a procedure would run contrary to the development of the Church's faith. In effect, it would amount to appealing from the faith of the Church to texts that are very close to Jesus, it is true, but nonetheless incomplete, since "the Church does not draw her certainty about all revealed truths from the holy Scriptures alone" (*Dei Verbum*, no. 9). Furthermore, it would be tantamount to regarding the contributions of *the history of the Church* and of the development of the faith, ultimately, as mere and even harmful additions that the institution accumulated like layers of sediment, rendering unrecognizable the stratum of the original message.

We should note here that the academic discipline of history as it investigates the *sources* of the Christian phenomenon only partially coincides with the theological method of faith, which is directed toward the divine *Source*. The similarity in terminology conceals a fundamental difference in approach. Although it is legitimate for objective observers of Christianity and historians of the early Church to consider the New Testament texts as primary *sources* and *data* and to treat them accordingly, catechists, in contrast, cannot limit themselves to this perspective. Indeed, the *Source* of the faith, as understood especially by the Council of Trent and Vatican II, is not identical with the texts of *Scripture*. This remark by Joseph Ratzinger is of capital importance and completely justified. It is of capital importance because it allows us to discern the hidden basis for a certain number of methods leading in some cases to an *evangelism* that sets Jesus up as a marginalized, prophetic figure, confronting or even opposing the institutional Church. These approaches are certainly not new in the history of the Church; the Church Fathers have already commented on them, and the Councils subsequently condemned what was erroneous in them. But are we not seeing a resurgence of these ideas in our day? The important thing now is to renew that spirit of critical reflection which is legitimately based on the very structure of the faith. Indeed, everything hinges on the concept of *Gospel* (a concept that Cardinal Ratzinger, in his conference, replaces with that of *revelation*, citing the great thirteenth-century Doctors of the Church). It appears to me that the term *Gospel* is at least equally suited to our present discussion; Yves Congar, Walter Kasper, and Ratzinger himself have treated this question in a pertinent way. When the Fathers of the Council of Trent, and later those of Vatican II, use the term *Gospel*, they give it a fullness of meaning and assign to it a much broader significance than the one that we attribute to the same word today. The *Gospel*, so understood, of course includes the four Gospels and the other New Testament writings, as well as the Old Testament as read in light of the New; but the *Gospel* refers also to the revelation of grace, which is like a gospel written, not on parchment, but directly on hearts by the Spirit of God. This *Gospel* living within the Church is the unique source of all salvific truth and of all moral discipline. Surely the great master of Tübingen, J. A. Möhler (1786–1838), whom Joseph Ratzinger cites in his conference, was the one who expressed most profoundly this way of looking at it.

The Gospel is the complete doctrine of Christ, the *kerygma* that was proclaimed orally, before and concurrently with the Gospel that was set down in writing. The two were created at the same time, but the *Gospel* is in the first place inscribed on the hearts of believers. As an excerpt from the living Word that had been proclaimed and heard, the *Gospel* took on a *permanent form* in the Gospels, which however do not exhaust the living *Gospel*. Möhler calls the *Gospel* that is proclaimed in the Church, and is present thanks to the Holy Spirit, tradition.[9]

So it is clear now that only this living *Gospel*, in the comprehensive sense, is capable of constituting the Church and of serving as her original *Source*. Consequently, this function can be claimed neither for *Scripture alone* nor for any doctrinal definition of the Church, taken by itself. Thus the term *Source* appears in its properly theological sense, the one that is very precisely attributed to it both by the Council of Trent (Session IV, 1546) and by the Second Vatican Council (*Dei Verbum*, nos. 7, 9).[10]

IV. Text and Commentary

Consequently, placing faith in the *Gospel*, understood in this way as the *Source* of the faith, can be understood only as a universal attitude of loving assent to everything that the Church offers us from her heart, whether it is a matter of Scripture, tradition, or the Magisterium. In this nurturing *environment*, catechesis unfolds by developing in those who participate in it a genuine *love for the Church*, which is

[9] The passage is a summary of the discussion by Möhler in sections 14–16 of *Die Einheit der Kirche*, ed. Geiselmann (1957), pp. 44–54.

[10] Ibid.; Yves Congar, *La Tradition et les traditions* (Paris: Fayard, 1963), p. 209.

inseparable from the love of Christ. At the same time, there will be a greater chance that the message will be presented in its entirety, and there will be less danger of choosing arbitrarily among the truths of the faith or of interpreting those same truths according to one's personal opinions. In this regard we have good reason to cite section 11 of the Decree on Ecumenism of Vatican II, while taking care not to misunderstand it. The text reads: "When comparing doctrines with one another [Catholic theologians] should remember that in Catholic doctrine there exists an order or 'hierarchy' of truths, since they vary in their relation to the foundation of the Christian faith." There is encouragement here for ecumenical dialogue, which could be extended to catechesis, provided that the *hierarchy of truths* is not mistakenly thought to mean that some of these truths can be forgotten or allowed to remain dormant, even provisionally, so as to insist on certain other truths that are easier to *present* or *believe*. Conversely, the *hierarchical ordering* of these truths will show the organic unity of the message centered on the Paschal Mystery of Christ, to which all the other truths must be referred in order to be understood fully.

Must we conclude, from the *internal cohesion of the Word and the organism that conveys it*, that the catechist would have no opportunity for initiative, no freedom, no say as to what is pedagogically appropriate, and that he would have to abide strictly, for example, by the plan that is already given in the Apostles' Creed? Quite the contrary. You will have noticed that Cardinal Ratzinger cites three times the important document drawn up by the French Bishops' Conference.[11] In it the French bishops express their conviction

---

[11] Conférence épiscopale française, *La catéchèse des enfants: Texte de référence* (Paris: Centurion, 1980).

that authentic catechesis will simultaneously "illuminate and criticize the spontaneous approach that children can make to the Truth that is proposed to them. Moreover, it can bring to light the original manner in which Revelation took place.... Catechesis can lead to Christ only if it respects the language by which he declares and conceals himself at the same time.... Thus the manner in which revelation provides the norm for the faith will be more evident" (no. 222, pp. 46–47).

This fundamental and essential citation explains precisely why the catechist is allowed to discern, depending on the individuals whom he is addressing, what approach, what method, what way of presenting the content of the faith will be most suitable. The apostolic exhortation *Catechesi tradendae*, which Pope John Paul II wrote[12] following the Synod of Bishops in 1977, had already dealt with the question of the relation between scrupulous respect for the integrity of the content and the method of presenting it, which will always vary. Indeed, *Catechesi tradendae* emphasizes that, depending on the situation,

> reasons of method or pedagogy [may] suggest that the communication of the riches of the content of catechesis should be organized in one way rather than another. Besides, integrity does not dispense from balance and from the organic hierarchical character through which the truths to be taught, the norms to be transmitted, and the ways of Christian life to be indicated will be given the proper importance due to each. It can also happen that a particular sort of language proves preferable for transmitting this content to

[12] John Paul II, *Catechesi tradendae*, October 16, 1979, reprinted in *Vatican Council II: More Postconciliar Documents*, ed. Austin Flannery, O.P. (Northport, N.Y.: Costello Publishing Company, 1982), pp. 762–814.

a particular individual or group. The choice made will be a valid one to the extent that, far from being dictated by more or less subjective theories or prejudices stamped with a certain ideology, it is inspired by the humble concern to stay closer to a content that must remain intact. The method and language used must truly be means for communicating the whole and not just a part of "the words of eternal life" and "the ways of life". (no. 31)

Of course, these observations are not new, but it is of some interest in the present situation to emphasize that the Catechism of the Council of Trent had already noted the basis for them: "But, as in imparting instruction of any sort, the manner of communicating it is of highest importance, so in conveying religious instruction to the people, the method should be deemed of the greatest moment." [13] The preface to the *Catechism of Trent* contains other remarks that Cardinal Ratzinger has already echoed, remarks that are worth citing again: "Age, capacity, manners and condition [of those being instructed] must be borne in mind. . . . The priest must not imagine that those committed to his care are all on the same level, so that he can follow one fixed and unvarying method of instruction to lead all in the same way (*aeque*) to knowledge and true piety. . . . The instruction is to be so accommodated (*accommodari*) to the capacity and intelligence of the hearers." [14] An approach, therefore, that takes into account the twofold need for stability and development. The instruction should be anchored in the central themes that summarize and define catechesis. Yet there should be room for development with a view to the

---

[13] *Catechism of the Council of Trent*, trans. and notes by John A. McHugh, O.P., and Charles J. Callan, O.P. (New York: Wagner, 1943), preface, question 11, p. 7.

[14] Ibid., pp. 7–8.

ability of a child or an adult or a group of persons to assimilate and comprehend what is taught. One single concern should guide the catechist: respect for the integrity of the message and the search for a suitable way of presenting it. In the movement back and forth between these two needs, the dialectic between *text* and *commentary* comes to life and takes shape. If there is nothing but a text—something unique, mandatory, and *closed*—it cannot be transmitted according to the laws of the human mind and of interpersonal communication. On the other hand, if there is nothing but commentaries, which are indefinitely *open*, changeable, and arbitrary, then no stable proclamation of the faith remains. No presentation of the faith can dispense with this requirement: to develop a commentary that is faithful to the text and, at the same time, to turn the text, by means of the commentary, into a living word that is appropriate and accessible to those for whom it is intended.

The catechist who is inadequately informed about the history of Christianity could tend toward the dangerous dichotomy that the *Texte de référence* by the French bishops was specifically designed to overcome. It would be a betrayal of the Christian message to present it under two separate aspects: on the one hand, a truth subsisting in a *pure* state in a few testimonials taken out of context and, on the other hand, *free* experiences or adaptations without any intrinsic coherence with the message. On the contrary, the catechist's *commentary* will also have to be rooted in the reality to which the *text* bears witness. It will do so, no doubt, in a *different* manner, but in profound agreement with the *text*. Actually, since the time when the faith was put into words, it has known several modes of presentation, which the faith itself suggests: narrative accounts, signs, commandments, conceptual reflection, ethical examination, celebration, and prayer.... We need only to look at the biblical genres or the great literary forms of expressing the faith in the past or the present age in order to be convinced and impressed by them in turn and to apply them.

Cardinal Ratzinger's insistence on the *four central components* of the *text* (Creed, sacraments, Our Father, Ten Commandments) should not be understood as a disparagement of the *commentary*, which attempts to correspond to the inexhaustible riches of revelation *with new expressions, in ever-changing situations*. Yet there is no denying that a period of fixation on the text has given way, at least in the Western world, to a period in which the commentary is so predominant that one does not really notice that it is commenting, because people *no longer know what it is commenting on*. Although these commentaries may be excellent for generations that had previously or in some other manner assimilated the *text* (the Creed), to the generations without preliminary formation it will seem that there are no pegs on which to hang them. This is the problem: the frequent lack of an initial contact and a primary transmission keeps the commentary from unfolding effectively. It fails to *connect* because there was no hook-up in the first place.

V. Formulas or Nuances?

Our examination of the questions raised by Cardinal Ratzinger's conference points out how ruinous it would be to indulge in facile contrasts between content and method, doctrine and experience, text and commentary, dogma and history.... It is one of the current tasks of Catholic theology, and of catechesis as well, to consider simultaneously both terms of these false alternatives. Thus the *method* is not unrelated to the *content*, from which it is, in certain respects, inseparable. Revelation is history; it is expressed mainly by the narrative *account* to which it is obliged *to return continually* by the very structure of the Gospel (which is indissolubly proclamation and narration). It follows that narrative [*le récit*] constitutes *one of the fundamental modes of communicating the faith today.*[15] There is no good reason, either, for setting the *Bible* in opposition to *dogma*, as though the Creed could in the least bit dispense us from the obligation of consulting the Old and New Testament, or, conversely, as though the Gospel accounts had not been clarified by the doctrinal formulas developed later by the Church (for instance, the doctrine that Christ is *true God and true man*).

Similarly, a *tenet of the faith* cannot acquire significance in a particular conscience and a concrete life unless it *fructifies* a *personal experience* by *overtaking* it and being wedded to it, at least partially. This does not mean, however, that the Word of life that God speaks to us is *identified* with the elements that already make up our experience. The Word remains *in front of* the believer and never stops being that "call that continually draws him farther in his search for his Lord".[16]

Finally, one cannot pit the *text* against the *commentary*, either, while overlooking the dialectic relationship and nourishing bond between them, which justifies them both. In setting up such an opposition, one would certainly run the risk, first, of confining the text to the position of an untouchable absolute, a sanctuary dangerously detached from history and life. For history, too, has shaped the text and enables it to be understood even today in terms of the

[15] Conférence épiscopale française, *Catéchèse des enfants, texte de référence*, no. 2221, p. 47.
[16] Ibid., no. 2222, p. 50.

task that it accomplishes in time, by the will of God. Now, in its various forms—Creed, sacraments, Lord's Prayer, Ten Commandments—the text in and of itself calls for the commentary, because "Christian truth never exists in a pure state." This is not to say that "it is presented with a fatal admixture of error, but rather that it is always imbedded in contingent notions and schemas and that it is not possible to isolate it from them." [17] It is clear, then, that the complete "liberation" of the commentary—for example, leaving it up to sheer creativity—leads to equally serious misunderstandings. For then it is being forced to compensate for the alleged rigidity of the text. The latter, consequently, no longer guarantees a living presence but finds itself reduced to a mechanical device for fulfilling externally the minimum requirements of an impoverished *orthodoxy*. The *General Catechetical Directory* of 1971 emphasized the "great demands [that] are being made on the ability and genuine Christian spirit of catechists.... It is their responsibility to choose and create the appropriate conditions for the quest of the Christian message, for its acceptance and for deeper study of it" (no. 71). The faith is handed on only by believers whose faith is alive.

With the exception of several incisive *expressions*, not one of the statements that Cardinal Ratzinger has made is missing from the documents that we have cited at length: the dogmatic constitution *Dei Verbum* of the Second Vatican Council, the *General Catechetical Directory* (1971), the apostolic exhortation *Catechesi tradendae* (1979), and the document by the French bishops on the catechesis of children (1979). One question remains for us to answer: What do

---

[17] Henri Bouillard, *Conversion et grâce chez saint Thomas d'Aquin* (Paris: Aubier, 1944), p. 220.

the doctrinal perspectives presented by so many authoritative voices tell us about the concrete practice of catechesis in our country? It was not the Cardinal's purpose to arouse doubt or to express mistrust or suspicion. Rather, he has asked us, it seems to me, whether the various sorts of pedagogical methods that are made available today to children and catechists are enough to accomplish the Church's mission in this critical area. There are, to be sure, many signs that real progress has been made, in circumstances that are often difficult for those who bear this heavy responsibility, and the laborers in this field deserve the thanks of the entire Church. Yet who could be completely satisfied with the manner in which, here in France, the adult generations are handing on the faith to children and adolescents? Could this question ever be irrelevant?

Difficulties in Teaching the Faith Today

Interview with Joseph Cardinal Ratzinger

Question: It would be taking owls to Athens[1] if we were to act as though the Church today were confronted for the first time with problematic questions about teaching the faith. The literature on this subject—at least here in Germany, which is representative of the situation in all so-called advanced industrialized societies—has been legion since the Second Vatican Council. The difficulties in teaching the faith are undisputed. All of those involved are affected by it, as well as the process itself. The old system of anchoring faith instruction at four places no longer works: it used to be oriented toward "content" [*intentionale*], that is, methodical verbal instruction, and "praxis" [*funktionale*], that is, the participation of those receiving instruction in prayer and worship (liturgy and sacrament), with these two modes taking place both publicly (in the parish, school, and kindergarten) and also privately (in the family). In order to overcome the difficulties in teaching the faith, does it make sense to keep analyzing the spirit or demon of the age and to try new experiments in an effort to outwit it, or should we say, realistically, that for the moment nothing can be done about it? We just have to get through these times.

---

[1] The owl was the emblem of the ancient city, so taking owls to Athens would be the equivalent of carrying coals to Newcastle.—TRANS.

Certainly in the future there will again be times that are more suitable for effective and lasting instruction in the faith.

Cardinal Ratzinger: The Church would most certainly not be fulfilling her mission if she decided to wait around for better times; with passivity of that sort she would instead be hindering their arrival. Besides, I would not view the various paths that you have spoken about as simple alternatives. Observing and analyzing the present age is certainly indispensable. "Being all things to all men", which Paul regards as an intrinsic requirement of apostolic service, includes a certain identification with other people that demands, first of all, becoming acquainted with them. Paul was able to become the "Apostle of the nations" because he not only had a thorough command of the Jewish theology and piety of his time, but was at home also, being a Jew of the Diaspora, in the thought patterns of the enlightened Greek-speaking Mediterranean world. Thus in his letters we find quotations from Greek poets and rabbinical forms of argumentation side by side. The decisive thing, of course, was that he did not simply go along with others or speak in flattering words; he did not try to win over anyone with cleverness—as he expressly emphasizes, for example in 1 Thessalonians 2:4–6—but rather his heart was filled with faith in Christ and with love for him "who loved me and gave himself for me" (Gal 2:20). Only conviction convinces, and it still does today. And so I would say that the first prerequisite for effective instruction in the faith is the catechist's own living faith, which also enables him to find ways to communicate his conviction to others. In that process, now as before, the paths that you have spoken about are interrelated. The French bishops have emphasized this very forcibly in a foundational document, *La catéchèse des enfants* [The catechetical instruction of children] (Le Centurion, 1980): Catechesis requires a text, understanding, and learning; it requires a connection with the liturgy, and it requires the communion of fellow believers. The fact that the family, albeit the basic unit of such a living faith community, often no longer performs this service nowadays makes it all the more the responsibility of the parish to offer such opportunities for shared faith.

Question: First let us look at those who are involved in the process of teaching the faith. Teaching the faith, in the narrow sense, is a process that takes place between a person who teaches and a person who is taught, whereby the community of the faithful should also support this process and share responsibility for it. Is it right to demand that the instructor should not only know the contents of the faith but also should himself believe them and, as it were, convey them to his listeners through his profession of faith?

If this is not only desirable but urgently necessary, by the very nature of catechesis, then what prerequisites must be established so that this demand can be fulfilled? We know that today many teachers and catechists have difficulty with the mysteries of the faith and that this is not always their fault—for instance, when because of the *numerus clausus*,[2] they chose religion as their major and also received a canonical mission [to teach], without having a real relationship to questions of faith. But even among those catechists who because of their closer ties to the Church deal very seriously with the questions of teaching the faith, it has not

[2] This is a system at German universities limiting the number of students who may specialize in a particular subject to the number of teaching jobs that will be available to them upon graduation.—TRANS.

been clearly determined whether or not instruction in the faith should be preceded by the presentation of information upon which faith instruction can build.

After all—and we turn now to the student, the one to be instructed—the youngster is at no time a blank page. In every case, at the point in time when the instruction begins, there has already been an education in the family and the wider milieu. We know what a great number of direct and indirect educators there are today, especially of those who distort almost everything that has to do with faith and religion, who keep it out of sight and therefore out of daily life, who erect blockades that are not so much the result of a deliberate intention as they are something inherent in those educators. Their law is function and functionality. In such an educational situation, can the Christian doctrine of salvation be communicated directly, solely in faith and with hope and trust in the Holy Spirit, or must we really go with a new approach?

Cardinal Ratzinger: Your first question is answered by what we have already said. Only someone who is himself a believer can lead others to the faith. Someone who cannot or can no longer believe must in all honesty relinquish this duty. It is a somewhat different question whether in our contemporary school system there are situations in which the explanation of the faith must be prepared from afar, so to speak. The problem of whether religious instruction in the schools should not simply turn into the providing of information, pure and simple, while relegating all sacramental preparation to the so-called Parish Religious Education Program, was the subject of a lively debate in the 1970s, especially in connection with the [World] Synod [of Bishops on catechesis in October 1977]. During those discussions it became clear that there are things that one really cannot speak about in a purely informative manner: every attempt to inform contains a dose of interpretation as well, and even apparent neutrality is actually a way of taking a stance with regard to the content in question. The gospel is more than (good) "news". It is (glad) "tidings", or a "message" that, as the contemporary philosophy of language puts it, has not only an informative but also a "performative" effect, which means that it intends to intervene in the existential situation of the listener and to change it; only when this has happened has the message "arrived" or been received at all.

This does not exclude, however, the possibility of making one's way little by little, stepwise, to the heart of this message; after all, that is what the early Christian catechumenate did. We know that in that process instruction about the core of the *mysterium*—the Eucharist and its basis in the Paschal Mystery—was reserved until the celebration of baptism during the Easter Vigil, which was often preceded by a catechumenate lasting several years. This time served as an initiation into the Christian community and was occupied to a great extent with moral instruction, to which the corresponding steps in life were supposed to conform. Lessons were drawn from the Wisdom tradition of Israel, which is why the Book of Sirach acquired the title "Ecclesiasticus" (the Church book)—it was the most accessible reading from Sacred Scripture throughout this period of training. In addition there was the Stoic intellectual heritage, in a Christian interpretation, of course, yet in this way there was still an appeal to reason, which was led on step by step. Today we, too, must recognize once more the importance of this moral education and of a supportive community that deliberately runs contrary to the standards that are taken for granted by the surrounding milieu, and we must draw the appropriate conclusions. In this sense I would agree with you, that we must "go with a new approach" with regard to the levels and steps of catechesis, precisely in order to preserve what is lasting.

Question: Quite early in the history of the Church it became evident what significance was attributed to the question: How can knowledge about the faith be communicated in an effective and lasting way? With the possible exception of the Middle Ages, questions about methodology played a major role in teaching the faith. This resulted in the creation of a special academic field. If one is convinced of the importance of these efforts since Augustine's time, then this presupposes that the core of the material, of the knowledge to be communicated, is undisputed; that the Church's deposit of faith, as tradition understands it, is believed and lived by all who teach, or at least that this is desired. Today we can no longer take it for granted that that is the case. One gets the impression that, as the consensus among instructors concerning the central questions of the faith weakens, the question of instructional methods increasingly gains importance. Is it true? As though they expected that the right method, suited to the spirit of the modern age, could compensate for the lack of consensus in questions of faith?

Cardinal Ratzinger: I must confess here that my knowledge of the actual situation of catechesis in Germany is limited, so that I cannot give any conclusive information on the subject. But an excess of method with respect to content has certainly been an established fact in the last twenty years. Of course this is not limited to religious instruction; one would have to say in this regard, rather, that a general development spread to religious instruction and drew it along in its wake. There was a continual tendency to make everything "scientific"; behind this there was a particular anthropology and an overall understanding of reality. Religious instruction, which by its very nature is directed toward mystery and involves the whole man, not just the understanding, suddenly found itself in danger of becoming an entirely foreign body within the "scientized" school, which would sooner or later lead to the loss of its place therein, unless it likewise assumed all the characteristics of a modern "academic subject". So it must have been a challenge for the catechists to show that religious instruction can be thoroughly structured as a "curriculum", just like every other subject—that it can be presented in the modern methodological package. It is plain to see that method, in this context, is no longer the path indicated by the subject matter itself (as Aristotle defined it); rather it becomes the instrument by which the object is tortured (a procedure that Francis Bacon considered sensible). By means of such "scientizing", the schools were supposed to do away with "manipulative" education completely and, through a purely informative process, to give the child the chance to develop in complete freedom. It is becoming increasingly clear that such "objectivity" was in truth an inhumane procedure. This system reached its utmost potential, so to speak, when religious instruction, too— which is essentially "education" and the integration of the human being in his totality—assumed the same form. Such a dictatorship of methodology is in fact a dictatorship of extraneous content. Where such a definition of school prevails, religious instruction must oppose the school's claim to authority, not only in order to remain true to itself, but also to protect man. In this whole process, no doubt, the contemporary crisis of faith played a decisive role. To some extent the process became possible only through this crisis, while to some extent it compounded and exacerbated it.

Question: Are there grounds for saying that theological pluralism in the Church today is also making a distinct impression on the practice of teaching the faith? Or—and let us take, for example, only those catechisms presently in use in the Federal Republic of Germany—are modern books about the faith only a reflection of theological opinions, as in all other ages, in which, as everyone knows, there were theological schools with opinions that appeared in faith instruction as well? Is the variety of theological opinions today of an essentially different quality than the earlier formation of schools? How does pluralism today compare with the pluralism of past ages—it being understood that by pluralism we do not mean theological differences of opinion about particular questions or pluralism in the sense in which Karl Rahner uses the term, which will exist for as long as men live, due to human limitations, but rather a pluralism analogous to Harold Joseph Laski's concept of pluralism (1915), which implies that the Church, like the State, is one association among many, which may not demand from her members more loyalty than the other associations, whereby the authority of the governing board to make a final decision as well as its right to obedience are rejected?

Cardinal Ratzinger: By her very nature, the Catholic Church can never accept Laski's concept of pluralism, as you have described it. After all, by definition she is a communion of faith. If this bond is dissolved, then other bonds step in to replace it—bonds that no longer arise from a common preexisting datum (the Bible as lived and interpreted in the

Church), but rather are based on the arbitrary will of the group. When that happens, other factors, for example political or other social decisions, become imperative, but these clearly can only be "particular" and thus have as their consequence the disintegration of the universal Church community. But you are right in saying that the binding character of the Church's Magisterium is less and less often accepted. That means that the boundaries between theology and faith are becoming increasingly blurred, that Church teaching is disappearing and theological teaching remains as the sole form of interpreting the Christian message. But then the pluralism of academic theological constructs becomes an end in itself, which obscures and displaces the unifying character of Church teaching; the only unity that remains then is something vaguely distant and unutterable, but it no longer has a concrete expression. This, too, is related to the scholarly and "scientific" tendency that we described before: the Magisterium now appears—in contrast to a theology that is understood in purely academic terms—as a power that is foreign to science, with which an institution is trying to interfere with the progress of science in a methodologically incorrect way. Neo-Marxist interpretations of what is going on are then within easy reach.

I think that yet another factor certainly plays an important role here, namely, the increasing plausibility of a purely congregationalist understanding of the Church. Hansjürgen Verweyen recently gave a stimulating account of the Puritan roots of Christianity in the United States in its early form, with its opposition between "Papism" and Anglicanism.[3] According to this understanding, all salvific power

---

[3] Hansjürgen Verweyen, "Die Situation der Kirchen und Religionen in den USA", *Internationale Katholische Zeitschrift* 12 (1983): pp. 144–54.

comes so directly "from above" that mediation of it through material or interpersonal realities is not possible. That means, then (as Verweyen demonstrates), that all ecclesiastical order has its origins from below, from the individuals who are saved and from their free associations. It seems to me that the average Christian consciousness today is almost universally determined by a somewhat coarsened form of congregationalist thinking: according to this consciousness there is, first, Christianity as such, and then—because human things require institutions—we must find for ourselves an organization in which it can continue. Thus the Church is regarded as an institution that, while necessary, given the conditions of human existence, is nevertheless organized by men alone and that is ultimately something external as compared to the contents and hence must not interfere in those contents as well. There is no need for a lengthy proof that, with such presuppositions, the contents of the Christian message itself will end up evaporating more and more and become thoroughly arbitrary. But given such a state of consciousness, which is fostered by widespread and plausible habits of thinking and living, it is very difficult to demonstrate the manifest character of ecclesiastical tradition, without which that tradition cannot be lived out. That, therefore, is what we should be concerned about above all else; then the concept of pluralism, too, will automatically fall into its proper place again.

Question: Preparation is needed if effective instruction in the faith is to be made possible today: preparation of the participants, preparation of the "materials" that are to be communicated. Yet where is the limit beyond which we can no longer speak of teaching the faith as a commission from and according to the mind of the Church? What does it mean today to say that this Bible history and that catechism are theologically correct? A non-fictional example: Is it crossing the boundary of what is permissible when, in order to makes things more comprehensible, exegetes set about "preparing" the Old and New Testament for this purpose. They no longer have the Old Testament begin with the creation of the world, because, after all, nobody was around then who could have witnessed it; instead they begin with the call of Moses, and not until the Book of Kings do so-called wise men "remember" the creation of the world. Furthermore they do not allow the New Testament to begin with the genealogy of Jesus or the Annunciation and the Nativity of our Lord; rather, it begins with the Acts of the Apostles, in which, by means of flashbacks, the young faith communities "remember" the life and deeds of the Lord. Again: Are such adaptations permissible?

Cardinal Ratzinger: There are many reasons worth considering for the catechetical trend of starting the Old Testament with something other than creation. To begin with, there is the view, which has been increasingly emphasized by exegetes in recent decades, that the internal beginning of the Old Testament is to be found, not in a belief in creation, but rather in the reality of the covenant. Gerhard von Rad has singled out Deuteronomy 26:5–9 as probably the oldest formula for Israel's profession of faith and has tried to demonstrate how the entire Old Testament grew up, as it were, around this basic creed. Corresponding, then, to this notion of the internal growth of Israel's faith were the literary-historical findings, which classified Genesis 1, in particular, as a relatively late text because of its literary form. The idea was to trace in catechesis these intrinsic steps of God's pedagogy and to build up the faith in a similar manner from the events of revelation, so as to lead up then to the belief in creation. There were other, additional pedagogical considerations, especially the fear that starting immediately with the creation account could bring the conflict between faith and science into catechesis at the very beginning and cause it to become an insuperable obstacle for all further progress.

It might be interesting to add here parenthetically that there were very similar deliberations in the age of the Reformation as well. The theological textbook of the Middle Ages, the so-called *Sentences* of Peter Lombard (d. 1160), had determined the order of the treatises in theology as follows: the triune God—creation and the fall—Christology and the doctrine of grace—the sacraments. When Luther framed the question of salvation in such radical terms, one consequence was that the systematic theologian of the Reformation period, Melanchthon, overturned this order and proceeded in a strictly anthropological manner in his textbooks from the years 1519 and 1521, emphasizing the theology of the covenant and of grace, without allotting a separate treatise to the Trinity or to creation. In 1535 he corrected this and returned again to the old order, and he stuck to this format in his last textbook from 1559.[4] For my part, now, I would distinguish the question of how the books of the Bible should be presented from the question of how a catechetical course should be structured. The Bible should be presented, in my opinion, as it is, and not as we are able to trace its internal and literary development with more or less probability.

Besides, as Claus Westermann has made clear, traditions about creation have accompanied Israel's faith journey from

---

[4] Cf. S. Wiedenhofer, *Formalstrukturen humanistischer und reformatoristischer Theologie bei Philipp Melanchthon* (Frankfurt, 1976), pp. 397ff.

the very beginning; they cannot be eliminated by abstraction from the image of the God of the covenant. They are at the same time the bridge that connects Israel's faith with the faith of the nations, even though Israel had to purify and reshape these traditions in many ways in light of its own concept of God. Therefore, in my own critique of this change in the sequence of biblical books, I would give somewhat different reasons from the ones you mention. First of all, it seems to me to entail an overestimation of historical hypotheses as opposed to the concrete Bible. The certified findings of exegesis are very valuable for a deeper understanding of the biblical message. Yet they cannot replace the concrete text; rather, they must instead remain an interpretation of and an introduction to them. Secondly, in the attempt to play down the idea of creation in favor of the idea of the covenant (and there is at least a danger of that reduction), I see a shift in emphasis in the entire structure of the faith, one that is not insignificant. It is not without good reason that the belief in creation stands at the beginning of the Apostles' Creed as well, because only in this belief does the belief in salvation attain its full greatness and depth. The creation account is not just an extension of the historical line, drawn back beyond Abraham to the earliest beginnings; it is a statement about the intrinsic importance of things, about the way in which reality itself is built, and as such it is indispensable. In today's crisis of technological progress, the necessity of a correct stance toward creation is amply clear, and at the same time this is a question about mankind's salvation. I think that it can be made clear to children, too, that the creation story is not some sort of naïve hypothesis about how the world came into being; rather, it is a qualitative statement about reality and about ourselves. Understood in this way, it should have high priority in catechesis, especially since it is not only a bridge to other religions, now as ever, but it also takes up the decisive question that reason asks about where being comes from, and hence it is extremely important in showing that the faith is reasonable.

I have difficulty in understanding the reversal in the sequence of New Testament books that you mentioned. Here the debate about the historical Jesus probably plays a role; that debate has only gone to show that a purely historical reconstruction of the figure of Jesus produces no convincing findings and thus none of the "collective certainty", either, that even Harnack expected from the historical investigation of the Bible. Because the historical Jesus became increasingly indistinct in this way, the only remaining point of departure for faith was the interpretation of him that the "community" had developed. The grain of truth in this is the fact that a Jesus who has been "scrubbed clean" of all faith, so to speak, and is discovered by means of a purely historical operation is a featureless figure. The scholar who proceeds in this manner, indeed, has to dispense with the real witnesses and the real experiences and go behind them to distill for himself better findings; any reasonable person could see that this does not lead to any satisfactory conclusion. But that does not mean that the faith should renounce its acquaintance with the real Jesus or stop speaking of the real events that took place through him and with him. The faith itself is an "eye"—the community of the Church claims, in its remembering, to know reality and not just to be describing its own consciousness. If someone does not accept this, then faith becomes a theory without any real content.

Of course, what I said earlier about the congregationalist understanding of Church, and about being enthralled by a particular notion of scientific method, comes into play again here. If the Church is only a way of organizing the faith that people themselves have chosen, but has in herself no other authority than that of the institutional structures that have been delegated to her by a group, then she can say nothing substantial at all, nor can she vouch for the history of Jesus. Then faith is reduced to theology, and then theology has no other certainty than that of historical hypotheses. In this case, indeed, there is only one way out: the desperate attempt to view the consciousness of the community nevertheless as a profound understanding of reality and thus, for what it is worth, to continue in operation. But in reality, one has thereby dismissed Christianity. The question about faith in creation is involved here, too: If creation is only an extrapolation from the idea of covenant, then the Virgin Birth, the miracles, and the Resurrection of Jesus, too, are just so many profound interpretations—in which case they cannot be events. But if they are not events, then what truth do such "interpretations" really have? What capacity do they have to carry the weight of human life?

I draw from this the logical conclusion that well-grounded teaching about the Church is absolutely fundamental. If there is such a doctrine, then we are justified again in starting with the reality of Jesus himself and in proclaiming the Jesus of the New Testament as the real Jesus. And this, in turn, is the prerequisite if Christian life is to maintain its identity.

Question: Although the emphases may have varied, the contents of the catechism were always the same: the Creed, the Commandments, the Our Father, the Hail Mary, the commandment to love God and neighbor. For a long time no one questioned the fact that the articles of the Apostles' and Nicene Creeds constituted the foundation of a catechism and catechesis. Is that still true today? Or does practical catechesis take its bearings from the widespread weariness among the faithful with regard to almost everything that you can call faith instruction in the strict sense? Now there can be no doubt that this weariness exists, a weariness that does not proceed from a protest against the "hard teachings" or from the arrogance of a *non serviam* [I will not serve]. Rather, it is the result of an inability and an unwillingness to understand, because the demand for a faith perspective is not satisfied by intellectual comprehension alone but takes other forms: experience, the subjective experience of spiritual awakening, movement, dynamism, fellowship among Christians, and saving the world through social service, all of that being driven by many irrational forces (as is almost always the case in the great movements of Church history), irrational factors that make everything we call teaching seem secondary. And if this is true—and you certainly share my opinion that irrational factors are the real driving force in the Church today—what happens, then, if this indisputably strong force spreads to the episcopate and the shepherds [*die Väter*], who are supposed to protect Church teaching but fail in this important duty because other tasks appear more important to them, or perhaps also because they no longer even understand that their most important task is to protect and foster and develop doctrine?

Cardinal Ratzinger: I am not as pessimistic as you. Naturally, I do not dispute the irrational factors that you are speaking about. They, too, at least in part, are the result of a proclamation of the faith that no longer has the courage to face reality. If the events of the New Testament can no longer be proclaimed as realities, but instead are presented as profound interpretations within the Christian consciousness, then, indeed, they themselves are already irrational factors, and then it is logical to resort, in a similar way, to irrational consolations in the midst of the world's cruelty. After all, a world whose origins we do not know is itself utterly irrational; only if matter comes from God's hands is it thoroughly rational. But if this is not the case, if everything is simply there, without reason, then rationality too is irrational, because it has no foundation in the totality of being. So the one thing causes the other here. In such a world, religion does not cease, since it is a primordial concern of man, but it then becomes what Karl Barth (incorrectly) described it as being: a flight from a substantial faith, which has become too difficult, into a never-ending search for the lost paradise. In this respect I think there is a call to a full, substantial faith precisely in the confusion and unhappiness of such experiences. That is the Church's opportunity at this hour.

My opinion of the episcopate, too, is more optimistic than yours. Naturally, bishops make mistakes; someone who is one himself knows that best. And of course they are children of their age, exposed to the pressure of the times, and again and again they will succumb to it for a stretch. Yes, the promise of remaining forever was given to the Church as a whole, and not to the bishops' conferences. But herein lies also the role of the primacy and of catholicity: no bishops' conference stands alone or subsists in and of itself; it is woven into the great fabric of Catholic life. As long as it remains within this framework, it will not make any decisions of ultimate importance without that unity, and certainly not contrary to it. It seems to me that the great significance of the Petrine office becomes visible here. It can help spread positive impulses; drawing upon the strengths of catholicity, it sets into motion mutual correction and itself embodies that catholicity. In saying that, I do not mean to fall into a false irenicism. The fact that there can be long-lasting periods of decline in the Church is, unfortunately, plain enough from history. Yet history also shows that the totality of the Church—which extends through the whole world and through all times and is held together and embodied by the Petrine office—bears within itself the powers of regeneration, so that it arises again and again from the dust to proclaim the message of salvation.

Archbishop Dermot J. Ryan (Dublin)

"Utter Mysteries from of Old" (Ps 78:2)

I stand before you as a former professor of Sacred Scripture and Oriental languages, now Archbishop of Dublin, and I am here to speak to you about "handing on the faith". I agreed to do so at the invitation of Cardinal Lustiger and Archbishop Decourtray, which was addressed to the ordinary of the Church of Dublin, and it is in that capacity that I accepted the invitation. Nevertheless, the Old Testament specialist in me led me to take the Word of God—a theme that is so rich—as my point of departure in dealing with the proposed topic. This will come as no surprise, I think.

The invitation to speak to you about handing on the faith was addressed to the archbishop of a great metropolis (which is grappling with the typical problems of such a setting—problems that concern you as well). No doubt you will be surprised at them. Ireland, after all, is a small country: the total population of the island is scarcely more than five million, of whom 3.5 million inhabitants are Catholics. And yet there are twenty-six dioceses. But the chief and troublesome peculiarity is the fact that the Diocese of Dublin alone includes 1,100,000 souls, one-third of the

Conference given January 8 and 9, 1983.

Catholics in Southern Ireland and 30 percent of the Church on the entire island.

Indeed, Dublin, the capital city of the Republic of Ireland and the seat of its government, has undergone a surprising expansion over the last thirty years, covering a broad geographical area in order to house ever-greater numbers of Dubliners. One could say that new parishes have sprung up on the countryside like mushrooms. In just a few years, pasture lands have become the site of thriving communities gathered around their pastors. The best indication of this rapid development is the following fact: Over the course of my ten years in the episcopate, I have personally consecrated forty-five new churches, ten of them in 1982, whereas during that same period I created fifty-four new parishes, increasing from 134 to 188 the number of these cultural subdivisions of my diocese.

To be sure, all of this brings with it a heavy financial burden, which falls entirely upon the members of the Church of Dublin. It is an even greater strain since these people have to provide not only for the construction of churches and rectories, but also in large measure for the building of parochial schools, and since they are responsible for contributing to the support of various services at both the parish and diocesan levels. Their generosity, born of their faith, manifests their ability to see beyond the parish environment and to view their diocese as a big family in which each member owes it to himself to take on part of the burden that belongs to all. We must recognize in this also the expression of their eagerness to hand on in turn the treasure of the faith that has come down to them from generation to generation, often at the cost of their ancestors' lives. And so, since parents residing in the older parishes have children who, when they marry, go to settle in the new

ones, they want to make available to them the same opportunities for prayer and the sacraments, for religious formation and membership in a vibrant faith community—
benefits they were already enjoying before.

Some of the reasons for this rapid expansion of Dublin
can be observed also in other large urban centers. For example, the rural exodus toward the city in search of jobs, the
growth of a central bureaucracy due to the presence of the
government, which seeks to surround itself with more and
more civil servants. Two factors, however, result from situations that are peculiar to Ireland and Dublin. First, there
is the slow decrease in emigration rates associated with the
increasing number of Irishmen who are returning to settle
in the country. Then there is the high birthrate, which is
indeed the highest in Europe. One consequence of this last
consideration: half a million people in our diocese, almost
50 percent, are less than twenty-one years of age. This throng
of young people, of course, offers great hope for our country, but it is easy to imagine the problems that it causes in
these times of economic recession in which we are hit hard
by unemployment.

At the same time, despite the greater numbers of build-
ings and priests, Dublin is experiencing the same disastrous
trends that afflict so many big cities in Western civilization.
The depopulation of downtown areas results in the deser-
tion of the parishes that are part of them; the churches,
often the most beautiful in the city, are left almost empty.
Young people and the not-so-young move to the new res-
idential neighborhoods, each to his own. The result is a
loss of ancestral wisdom for lack of contact between the
generations, the isolation of young families, especially of
young mothers who no longer or only with difficulty can
call on their own mothers for help. There is an overall

danger of a breakdown and disintegration of society. As for those who still live in the center of the city, their living conditions give rise to many pastoral concerns.

Add to all this that our people are allowing themselves to be ensnared by materialism and the desire for relative prosperity, which of course can be explained in part by the poverty we have endured for so long, until recent times. Consequently the Church is facing the growing problems of alcoholism, drug use, premarital and extramarital relations, the weakening if not the collapse of the home, dishonest business practices, and violence in the streets and even at the heart of political life.

In the past—a long but already far-distant past—Ireland was known as the island of saints and scholars. I am not at all sure that it still deserves that title. But we can say, at any rate, that by the very fact that it was an isolated island, it was often protected against pernicious influences from without. At least it slowed down their impact. But now, as a result of the pervasive and aggressive mass media and the ease of transportation, we have to confront the same polluted tidal wave that is submerging more highly developed centers with information of all sorts and is threatening the heritage of our faith.

As the bishop of such a large metropolis, I share therefore the concern of my brother bishops in Paris and Lyons about the need to make sure that the faith is handed on. Like them and with them, I too feel responsible for preserving and propagating the faith in Europe. In many respects, our continent is behaving like an old man, anxious about his comfort, his strength exhausted, with little hope for the future, almost forgetting a past that nevertheless could inspire young people. The many countries of the world that, in one sense, received the faith from

Europe might expect something better. As they build vigorous local Churches, they keep their eyes fixed on us, hoping to see the fruits of a centuries-old wisdom, of a deeply rooted strength, of a lofty spirituality that has been purified by long experience of alternating successes and failures.

Allow me to mention at this point in my speech that my presence here is not fortuitous. I am only adding a short paragraph to the already extensive history of cooperation between the Church of France and that of Ireland. It started, one might say, with Saint Patrick himself. Indeed, he prepared for his mission under the direction of Saint Germain of Auxerre. Everyone knows the success he had. Later the Irish, Saint Columban in particular, evangelized France in turn. As Archbishop of Dublin, I am happy to recall more particularly Saint Laurence O'Toole. He, too, was an Archbishop of Dublin, and he had to appear before the King of England, Henry II, who at that time was touring his lands in Normandy. He was cordially welcomed by the inhabitants of the town of Eu, but he took sick and could not return home and died there in 1180. Over his tomb they built a beautiful collegiate church. A testimony to the holiness of Saint Laurence, it expresses at the same time the faith and charity shared by our respective peoples at the turn of the thirteenth century.

At her height, the Irish Church expressed her faith through works of art. You can marvel at some of them—and not the least significant examples—by visiting the current exposition at the Grand Palais [in Lyons] entitled "Treasures of Ireland". The promise they held was unfortunately not borne out by what followed. Indeed, our land was denied the freedom to express its own genius in art and culture, a genius that the faith nevertheless enriched and deepened. In France, in contrast, you have been able to produce many master-pieces of literature, art, and architecture. The great cathedrals still bear witness not only to the talent and skill of those who designed and built them, but also to their understanding of creation, of the place of man in it, and of God's plan for his creatures.

Let us marvel at the work of our ancestors. Time and energy, skill, imagination, scarce materials, a variety of inspiration and a wealth of catechetical teaching—all this was placed at the service of God, the Creator and Savior of mankind. When we interrupt our hectic activities to admire these marvelous works, we should guard against looking at them solely from the perspective of the fine arts. They are also, indeed, the expression of a creative faith, of a concept of the world in which God and man are in a definite relationship to one another. These works of art also invite us to be impressed by them and to adopt their point of view, and it would be a mistake to reject this invitation because of their naïveté, as though they were incapable of communicating a message. Such an attitude would result from the blindness of modern men: so saturated are we with technology that we are positive that we have nothing to learn.

In the age when France was building her cathedrals, architectural and artistic achievements in Ireland were reduced to a more modest scale. Furthermore, with the systematic destruction of the monasteries in the sixteenth and seventeenth centuries, this activity was suddenly interrupted; the artists and artisans had to go into exile in order to escape death. Many of them took refuge in France.

Over the course of those gloomy centuries, furthermore, because of that destructive spirit, it became almost impossible to train priests in Ireland. A great number of Irish Catholics fled to France and to other countries on

the Continent in order to pursue their studies for the priest-
hood. They benefited from the hospitality of the so-called
Irish Colleges in Paris, Bordeaux, and Nantes. As they
prepared for their ordination, they knew that they could
very well be preparing for martyrdom, too. They did not
reject this prospect, so great was their faith, so much did
they want to witness to it in order to keep that faith from
dying in their persecuted land. Indeed, it was very hard to
live a life of faith there. Whereas in other places the rit-
uals were celebrated with great pomp in splendid cathedrals,
our ancestors were reduced to the essentials, and the sacraments were administered in haste under the vault of
heaven, whether on the hilltops or in the valleys, shel-
tered by thick forests. Although the sermon could not last
very long, these sacramental encounters had such an effect
on the Irish people that a very high level of Mass attendance has continued there to the present day. This is a
testimony to the love for Christ and the supernatural courage of these priests, who were ready to die so that the
faith might live on. It also expresses the awareness of Irish
Catholics that they can draw on the lessons from the past
by receiving the sacraments regularly. Indeed, their practice of their living faith enables them to read the signs of
the times, to deal with current events, and to hand on
what they themselves have received, despite the difficult
circumstances.

We can already draw several conclusions from this review
of some of the facts from our common history. Of course,
these conclusions are evident only to those who are not
content with reminiscing about a dead past full of successes
and failures but are also capable of meditating on them and
deriving a practical lesson from them. It is appropriate, however, to take a step even farther back. Let us return to my

first love, the Old Testament, and the source of the title I have given to this conference, namely, Psalm 78. In the first two verses the author already clearly defines the concern he has in mind:

> Give ear, O my people, to my teaching;
> incline your ears to the words of my mouth!
> I will open my mouth in a parable;
> I will utter mysteries from of old. (Ps 78:1–2)

And so the psalmist intends to explain the lessons of the past, so that the mighty deeds of God might be rendered intelligible, making possible the response that he awaits.

He does this, not only so that his contemporaries can conform their lives to the divine will, but also to help them pass on their insights to their children. Thus they will be encouraged to trust in God precisely because of the marvels he has accomplished on their behalf. Signs of God's love, they are an invitation to respond by keeping his commandments. These events from the past would teach young people how to avoid the mistakes of their rebellious, inconstant ancestors, and the generation to come would learn to put its faith in God—something their fathers had not done.

In these verses, you see, the psalmist develops a whole program for the people of God. Although this program concerns believers before the time of Christ, it applies just as well to those who believe in him. For it is true in any age that if the Church fails to remember, she ceases to exist; if she does not preserve the memory of the past, she is no longer alive; if she is cut off from her roots, she will wither away.

Why should the Church have to remember? The reason is that she and her history constitute a whole: one single being. From her very beginning, indeed, the Church of

Christ is history. She is rooted in objective historical facts, which distinguish her from the subjective creation of fertile imaginations. And so she was preceded by particular historical events, founded on the basis of historically observable deeds, and derives her identity from persons and statements that are well qualified for this purpose by their historical resonance. Thus the Church lives in continuity with her past. If the latter is disrupted, she loses her identity, she actually ceases to be the Church of Christ.

This being the case, certain things about the Church cannot be changed, because they spring from her historical origin. They happened once and for all, so that they are constitutive elements of the Church. The apostles and the early Church attributed such importance to them that they preserved them: some in Scripture (the Old and New Testaments), some in doctrine and in the liturgy, and others in institutions. They handed them on to be preserved in the Church just as they are: not as dead things, but rather as life-giving elements that guarantee the vitality of the whole organism until the end of time.

It follows that when we evangelize by preaching, catechesis, or theological reflection, these elements that are essential to our Church must be taught without adding anything. These facts, these truths, these fundamental realities, therefore, can be explained and understood only with reference to the historical context of the life of Christ and of the people of God. In one sense we will always have to accept them as coming from outside, from somewhere other than the nations, cultures, and civilizations that are distinct from the Chosen People. Indeed, they cannot be deduced or derived from any other society, religion, or philosophy. To alter these elements would amount to changing the identity of Christ's Church. Therefore they must be presented as givens—as a gift, for that is what they are. They must be handed down reverently from one generation to the next in order to correspond to Christ's will for his Church until the end of the ages.

All of this, again, leads us to declare that if the Church ceases to remember, by that very fact she ceases to exist. Consequently there is a long tradition of the Church reflecting upon her history, inquiring into her origins, her development, and her future. By a reflection of this sort, we, the members of the Church, can learn a lesson from the mistakes of the past; we can discover the riches hidden in it; we can make usable today resources of strength and inspiration that were hitherto unknown, rejected, unappreciated, or simply forgotten.

Of course, there is another excellent reason for the Church to remember: the Lord's command, *"Do this in memory of me."* This meant first that the Church was to keep in mind the Lord's words and actions, in their particular context. This then involved more general implications, because an understanding of the Eucharist presupposes an understanding of everything that Christ said or did.

It seems to me inappropriate to enter here into a discussion of the liturgical significance of "memory". Instead, I would like to offer a few remarks on the role of memory in catechesis. One could very well regard my observation as a lesson drawn from the recent past.

Not so long ago the catechism was a very important part of the work that was undertaken in order to pass on the faith from one generation to the next. We know, certainly, what its flaws were: the excessive and too exclusive reliance upon memorization. Questions and answers learned by heart required little or no understanding.

Recently, and especially since Vatican II, there has been a reaction against this procedure, and, as so often happens, it has led to the opposite extreme. Most of the time religious instruction requires scarcely any memorization or none at all. Some have gone so far as to encourage children to compose their own prayers, supposedly because the traditional formulas seemed too difficult and impossible for young minds to understand.

Memory work has fallen into disfavor across the board in education. But the consequences of such a method for the very identity of the Church have been so serious that I must recall several pertinent sentences from *Catechesi tradendae*:

> At a time when, in non-religious teaching in certain countries, more and more complaints are being made about the unfortunate consequences of disregarding the human faculty of memory, should we not attempt to put this faculty back into use in an intelligent and even an original way in catechesis, all the more since the celebration or "memorial" of the great events of the history of salvation require a precise knowledge of them? A certain memorization of the words of Jesus, of important Bible passages, of the Ten Commandments, of the formulas of key doctrinal ideas, etc., far from being opposed to the dignity of young Christians, or constituting an obstacle to personal dialogue with the Lord, is a real need, as the Synod Fathers forcefully recalled. (*Catechesi tradendae*, no. 55)

Quite obviously, an understanding of the contents of the faith is of considerable importance. On the other hand, we should not insist too much on this principle of comprehension. After all, who has a complete and exhaustive understanding of the Our Father, the Hail Mary, or the Ten Commandments? Yet the Christian who is willing to learn these formulas in his youth grasps and appreciates them better and better to the extent that he strives to live a deeper spiritual life, beginning with regular reception of the sacraments and the practice of the moral virtues. Moreover, if it should happen that someone strays far from the Lord's path, often he finds it again by following the tracks that were impressed on his memory during his childhood days.

Furthermore, we can observe how much young children—despite their awkwardness—love to be able to join their parents in reciting the Our Father at Mass. This is how youngsters become adults in Christ within the bosom of the ecclesial community and how they become heirs to the tradition.

Besides, the historical origin of handing on the faith, starting from unique events, necessarily implies a special, even technical language. Through these words and expressions (the original use of which may in fact not have been limited to the Christian context) a unique meaning and a connotation derived from the unique Christian context are transmitted by those who use them.

It goes without saying that this terminology of the faith must be explained from the outset. The essential truths that it expresses cannot always be grasped immediately, and perhaps they will never be thoroughly comprehended. There are certain parts of our prayers, worship, and doctrine that will always remain imperfectly understood and partially hidden: "For now we see in a mirror dimly" (1 Cor 13:12). This does not mean that we are excused from the duty of learning them and teaching them to the younger generations, since that is required to ensure the continuity and identity of the faith and, consequently, of the Church.

Besides, to say that the vocabulary of the faith seems too technical for youngsters to learn and therefore to teach is to disregard the ease with which they master the terminology of modern science. They know all about space travel and star wars; they enthusiastically play a whole series of new, extremely complicated games.

Then, too, with the passage of time, this terminology of the faith that is acquired in childhood will gradually make more sense. Indeed, a more developed religious awareness and the better understanding that results from it will make sure of that. Furthermore, these words that are sometimes so strange at the beginning will acquire a personal significance through the ups and downs of religious life.

It is clear, then, that these formulas of prayer, doctrine, and Christian life that ought to be learned are extremely important from the perspective of catechesis. They make up the core of the knowledge shared by all believers who are united by the same commitment to Christ. They are indispensable for the propagation and development of instruction in the faith. If, on the one hand, they are situated at the point of departure for that instruction, on the other hand, they provide a precise summary of all that has been said on the subject. Because they were convinced of this, the bishops of twelve German dioceses have just approved the publication of a manual of Christian doctrine, in which the faith is explained on the basis of the Apostles' Creed.[1]

When the official Eucharistic Prayers are well known, they too can provide material for doctrinal explanations and elaboration. In that way the faithful come to realize the wealth of their tradition and the profundity of their faith, which consist of knowing God and living a Christian life.[2]

---

[1] *Botschaft des Glaubens: Ein katholischer Katechismus* (Augsburg/Essen, 1980).
[2] Cf. The Bishops of France, *Il est grand le mystère de la foi* (Paris: Centurion, 1978).

Yet another lesson emerges from the recent past in which we have so often changed our way of presenting religion. Various catechetical methods have followed one another in all-too-rapid succession; each one, to be sure, had certain advantages, but none of them could claim to be the best. This sort of unhealthy exclusivity creates divisions between parents, catechists, and priests.

The kerygmatic approach was considered preferable to the apologetic method. Next we heard a lot about the history of salvation; then there was an anthropological approach and another thematic approach. All of that in turn was abandoned for a personalized or experiential presentation. You must admit: while the catechists are devoting considerable energy to discussing the respective merits of these methods, which are creating a certain confusion in the minds of their students, there is a real danger of losing sight of the essentials of the faith. Then continuity in teaching the faith and unity in presenting it are gone.

Our experience in Ireland seems to show that, despite our investment of time, energy, and money to produce very elaborate textbooks and cassette tapes, and even with well-trained catechists, many children leave our primary schools without knowing the basic prayers and the doctrinal points that are appropriate for their age. Likewise, the students who complete secondary school do not have the knowledge of the faith, of the principles of Christian morality, of the Church and the liturgy that one would expect of them after all the careful attention that has been showered on them. There are, of course, many reasons for this situation; people will allude to the potential of the individual student, the social environment, and his family background. At the same time, why not ask whether the core of the doctrine has actually been taught correctly? Has it been presented with sufficient clarity, insistence, and intelligence? Has a real effort been made to have the students learn the basic minimum that they will be able to use later on when they embark on their adult life as Christians?

Youngsters need to be provided with what one could call the principal landmarks in the territory of faith. These reference points will make it possible for them to stay on the right path while they are pursuing knowledge and experience in every direction. Young people, and even adults, will find in these sorts of milestones the help they need when they as Christians have to confront problems or obstacles in life.

Shortly after Vatican II, some confusion arose between the role of catechists and the role of theologians. Individuals with catechetical training thought that they had theological qualifications as well and that they could engage in controversies. During their formation they may well have become acquainted with current theological debates, yet without having received the necessary basic religious education. Afterward they discussed these matters in their classes and got their students involved in them, although neither the instructors nor the students had the resources to deal with such questions.

The inclusion of exploratory or experimental theological hypotheses in catechesis led to the same results. The danger is that both catechists and students end up drifting in confusion, with no idea of where they are. They are like people who want to climb Mount Everest without knowing how to get to the foothills or even how to read a map!

The opening verses of Psalm 78 emphasize the responsibility of parents in handing on the faith. In Ireland we are trying to carry out our duties in this regard in two ways. First, on the level of preparing textbooks for the primary schools: the role of parents is recognized as well as the roles of students and catechists. Then, when the time arrives for the sacramental celebrations, we make sure that there are family gatherings also and, if possible, events in the life of the parish community. Thus parents, catechists, and students work together in each parish, of course in close collaboration with the local clergy. In preparation for receiving the sacraments we plan a series of meetings, discussion sessions, pastoral visits and paraliturgical services, to which both the children and their parents are invited. The priests often find that, from the catechetical perspective, these preparations have greater impact when the faith and religious practice of the parents are reinvigorated, when they acquire a more structured understanding of the faith so that they themselves can help form their children.

In this whole endeavor we set great store by the parish. After all, it represents, does it not, the smallest apostolic unit, well suited to implementing locally the methods for handing on the faith.

The close collaboration among parents, catechists, priests, and students is facilitated in our dioceses by the integration of religious instruction in the school curriculum. This situation arose at the very outset from the parents' desire to have their children introduced simultaneously to the faith and to secular subjects, and we continue along these lines in order to comply with the wishes of the overwhelming majority of the families. Besides, in this way we are in agreement with the European Convention for Human Rights:

> No one can be deprived of the right to education. The State, in carrying out the duties that it assumes in the area of education and instruction, shall respect the right of parents to ensure that this instruction is in conformity with

their religious and philosophical convictions. (Article 2, Additional Protocol no. 1)

Therefore it should come as no surprise that our particular tradition, combined with the facilities we have available in the parishes and schools, assures that a great proportion of Catholics in Ireland continue to practice their faith. Average Sunday Mass attendance nationwide generally does not drop below 80 percent, and in many places it exceeds 90 percent. This does not mean that we do not have our own dark spots; these can be found especially in the more important urban centers.

Despite this high level of practicing Catholics, we cannot look on the contemporary scene with complete confidence. Apart from the constant pressure of materialism, which threatens the Irish as it does other peoples, we in Ireland perhaps need to reflect a little more on the best way of living out our faith. Christianity cannot be reduced to a formula to be learned or to cultural customs; it is also and more profoundly a form of interior life. From the earliest days of the Church this essential truth has been highlighted: the Acts of the Apostles call Christianity "the Way" (Acts 24:22). This would correspond with the Old Testament understanding of what the revelation offered to the people of God meant. They were unceasingly urged to keep the commandments because that was the only adequate response to the love God had for them.

We need to increase our ability to witness to our Christian faith in our everyday activities, in our personal relationships, in our homes, and in our workplaces. We have to realize how important it is not to shut ourselves off in a cocoon of piety but to work also for the genuine justice and charity that set us free from self-concern.

On the other hand, we should develop our capacity for reflecting on our faith so as to be able to give a reason for it (cf. 1 Pet 3:15). For we need to strengthen the intellectual foundations of our faith. It is important, therefore, that laymen have a formation that will prepare them to witness, according to their particular charism, to the Gospel and to Christ in those settings where they have the right and the duty to evangelize (cf. *Evangelii nuntiandi*, no. 70). They are called to preach the gospel, however, not necessarily directly, but indirectly, through their work and their way of life. And they can set about doing this in the assurance that they are not just proselytizing for a particular sect, but rather, on the contrary, that they are promoting the authentic, holistic humanism that the Holy Father [Pope John Paul II] tirelessly proclaims. Christian anthropology allows us to make this claim, because it seeks to conform itself to God's plan for the person he has created, a plan that we come to know through divine revelation and observation.

This whole process of handing on the faith, especially in these days in a big metropolis, proves to be extremely complex. It involves organization, the deployment of a lot of human and material resources. Although it concerns all the faithful, it is nevertheless incumbent upon only a few, whose burden is that much heavier.

In the heat of battle we must not become preoccupied with analyses, whether statistical, sociological, or psychological. We must not allow ourselves to be polarized by questions of method and curriculum. Are we not all obliged, as Christians, to acknowledge the part that the Divine Mystery plays in our actions? Not only the mystery that concerns the order of created things, but also the mystery pertaining to revelation and the growth of the Kingdom of God. We must respect the dynamism of the Spirit of Christ.

Ultimately, therefore, what do we do but plant and water? Here, as in nature, God gives the growth to the things he has created (1 Cor 3:7). Not even a bishop can exempt himself from this great rule of the faith.

There is no need to go into detail: at the heart of a great metropolis there is no lack of demands resulting from innumerable pastoral needs. It takes innovation and imagination to respond to these demands so as to offer the proper spiritual food to people with widely varying tastes. We thank God, therefore, with all our heart for having raised up small groups in the lay movements that, within our community, commit themselves to prayer and charitable works and theological reflection. They clearly deserve our help and encouragement if they are truly incorporated into the Church and if they labor with Christ, in his Spirit, for the building up of his Body.

Simply mentioning these many initiatives reminds us that alone we can do nothing and that God guides us all. For all are going about the difficult work of evangelization and handing on the faith. The divine assistance applies in the same way to every member of the Church. The Old Testament tells us this. Does it not give us the example of a long series of great religious leaders, prophets, priests, and kings? After God revealed himself to them in a privileged way, he sent them on a mission, and whenever one of them balked at taking up his burden, he reassured him, "I will be with you." Think of Moses, Isaiah, Jeremiah, and Ezekiel, not to mention all the others. Now Christ acts no differently with regard to his apostles and his Church. Does he not say: "I am with you always, to the close of the age" (Mt 28:20; cf. Acts 18:10)? Does he not promise that his Holy Spirit will sustain his Church, as her guide, her head, and her light, so that she can proclaim to the world the good news that he brought to mankind by his words and deeds (Jn 14:26; 15:26)?

Today Jesus continues to help us. He inspires those who preach his gospel, the ministers of his Church and of mankind. He gives others the strength to give witness in religious life. He enlightens and energizes lay people, since he fervently desires that they will be a light to the world, impart flavor to it, and arouse it from its materialistic slumber. As light, salt, and leaven, it is their duty to change their fellowmen by helping them to become aware of their true worth as created by God in his eternal Wisdom and redeemed by Christ in his infinite Love. Thus the Word of God is directed to everyone, in order to show them the way to true happiness, and it becomes the servant of all, so that each one's search may successfully reach its goal. Yet we, too, suddenly find that we are servants of this Word, inspired by the same fascinating Spirit; we proclaim him and, if we do not resist him, become instruments that the universal Love of God can make use of. May this reassure us in our faith and our hope. Far from wanting to control everything ourselves, let us not cease to entrust ourselves to God. The Word we have touched, by its own power, will also touch other human hearts through us.

But we must be careful! Working for God with faith in him as our motive requires a special expertise. Provided by modern science with a wealth of resources—especially technology, specialization, and planning—we must not forget that in order to use them in God's service we must never allow ourselves to be cut off from Christ. Therefore we cannot do without prayer and contemplation. Spiritual insight into reality—which is just as important as statistical studies—will be granted to us only if we call upon the Lord and meditate on his Word.

The Old and the New Testaments offer us their inexhaustible wisdom; a Christian ought not to neglect them. The Scriptures, indeed, place at our disposal the long history of a people that has not stopped living in the sight of God, permeated by the leaven of divine revelation. How could we not learn lessons from this extraordinary path of the Chosen People under the influence of the graces given to them over the centuries?

Do we not have to deal with the same human nature? The Old Testament describes it at length: the humanity that surrounded Israel, with which it lived in all sorts of tensions and exchanges, had the same desires as ours and was driven by the same passions. Guilty of similar mistakes, it gave itself over to the worship of similar idols. It is enough to mention Bacchus, Venus, and Mammon to be convinced that the attractions that turn us away from God remain unchanged. Their true worth was gauged long ago by the God of both Testaments, most often in the midst of tears and sometimes anger. Granted that we have allowed ourselves to be lulled into an excessive confidence in the power of our modern technology—to the point of believing that we can do without God—we should remember the experience of those technocrats who attempted to build the Tower of Babel (Gen 11:1–9). Addressing the problems inherent in big cities by no means requires that we ignore God: that would not help us at all.

Our position is not at all related to anti-intellectualism. It is not a question of a fundamentalist approach, any more than it is an unqualified approval for any and all forms of charismatic Christianity. Let each one be the judge of that. When I was teaching at the university, I came into contact with intellectuals and specialists and discussed with them their expectations and their ideological research. I was armed with the usual skills—one might say the technology—of a professor of Oriental languages and exegesis. Nevertheless my dealings with the people involved in the charismatic movement, for example, were never anything but cordial. For as I became acquainted with the way these people were living, I came to recognize the fundamental value of their enterprise.

Be that as it may, I think that the moment has come to take a comprehensive overview of the situation. The specialists and the experts cannot claim to have a monopoly on the truth. By what title? Marshall McLuhan himself declares that a specialist is "one who never makes small mistakes while moving toward the grand fallacy". This is not to say that we can do without specialists in the pursuit of knowledge. Indeed, they have their place, in the Church as well as in society. But they should know well enough to present their opinion only within the scope of their competence, since their point of view obviously remains incomplete. On that condition they can speak authoritatively. Among the immense crowd of Christians, the specialists and the experts, as well as all those who take on a special responsibility, have their place so that they can play their part better in this great musical ensemble and contribute more effectively to the success of the performance. But they will not find that place unless they are willing to avoid discord with the composer and the conductor, both of whom in this instance are God.

In this way, then, praying and meditating upon Scripture, attentive to the Spirit who speaks to us also through the voice of the Church, we will manage to learn from the past and "utter mysteries from of old". Then we will be in a position to hand on something valuable and living to our children, something we and they will be able to live by. This would be the correct response to the psalmist's request.

You will have understood even better what he means: We must now and will always have to avail ourselves of what has been spoken to us by God, by his Spirit, and by the Word: This Divine Word, as Saint John proclaims, this creative Word and guiding Law, this prophetic Voice and eternal Wisdom, "became flesh and dwelt among us. . . . And from his fulness have we all received, grace upon grace" (Jn 1:14, 16).

Reflection by Bernard Bro, O.P.

The Church in Ireland has paid dearly for the right to "utter mysteries from of old". Without raising his voice, Archbishop Ryan recalls "the sacraments ... administered in haste under the vault of heaven"; the priests who were condemned to exile or flight; the Christians who were "preparing for martyrdom". We would add that this was happening at that very time when the Catholic Church in France could afford educational institutions and an intellectual life, luxurious church furnishings, and even ideological disputes that, along with Jansenism, Gallicanism, and Quietism, sometimes seem to us now to be the whims of spoiled adolescents and also, alas, the twilight of faith.

Let us note here two lessons for our faith: his realism and his humility—both of them a source of greater understanding.

The Realism of Faith

Archbishop Ryan, though himself a specialist in Oriental languages and exegesis, has the quiet audacity to recall that, in the presence of mystery, specialists and experts do not have the last word. "A specialist is one who never makes small mistakes while moving toward the grand fallacy!" What a bracing call to realism!

We do believe, not in discourse about questionable events, but in the reality of these events. The fact that it is difficult to explain the "how" of this reality only makes more urgent the concern that goes beyond the hypotheses to grasp what

is real. This is a crucial point in all theology of faith: dem-
onstrating how our faith terminates, not in propositions,
enuntiabilia, but in reality.

The witness of the apostles is a historical fact and is
based on historical events. Although history does not exhaust
the facts concerning the life of the Risen One, these facts
are part of history. Every age has attempted to eliminate
the occurrence of the mystery and, at the same time, its
reality. Yet each time the mysterious event has proved to
be stronger than its opponents. One cannot tinker with
the Gospel texts and get away with it. They put up resistance to such treatment, and the testimonies are more consistent than the critics are sometimes willing to tell us.
The apostles see and they believe (Jn 20:29). They ponder
their doubts (Lk 24:37–42) because of the very reality they
perceive and run up against.

If the Word of God became incarnate, it was in order to
be visible, to be vulnerable, to be accessible in a new and
personal presence of God to men. If one were to reduce
the Incarnation to little more than a vague relationship to
the universe, if he were not the Body born of the Virgin
Mary and crucified under Pontius Pilate after all, then it
would be because God had only "loaned" us his Son! Not
only the texts or the theories lead us to affirm this realism,
but also the most profound elements in our faith. What
does faith claim? It says: God exists; he is a gift, and he lives
in us. This is likewise what is sung and said by every being
that loves. Someone who loves is transported into a world
with a reality surpassing everyday routine because the friend,
the beloved, the spouse does not merely live a physical life
extrinsic to the lover, but he lives within him and inflames
his heart. This presence is so essential that sometimes those
who love each other go so far as to say: "When you come

down to it, whether you are present or absent, you are always there." It is the same with the faith.

But something dangerous slips in here that can be deadly to the faith. One risks reducing this presence of God and of the mysteries of Christ to hypotheses that are more or less subject to our verification. When this happens, one simultaneously loses the sense of their reality, which is greater than our intellectual constructs and hypotheses. One must then return to what we would like to call *the realism of the Bride*. Archbishop Ryan emphasizes this very well when he recalls how the faith and the regular reception of the sacraments are intrinsically connected.

It is true that it is not enough for the beloved to be "elsewhere", if he is not internally present in my faith, in my heart, in my actions. But what good would it be to have within us the interior presence of someone who was no longer really alive? Let us look at how true lovers love, and we will understand the Christian faith. Does a wife not care about the return of her husband who is in prison, just because he lives in her heart? It is precisely the wife's realism that makes her want her husband to live at the same time in her heart *and* in her home. And to say that it is enough for her that he dwells in her heart is to say that, in fact, he does not dwell in her heart. The same realism demands that he also exist *really*, truly, that he be living now. The fact that Christ is already in his heart, in his life, in his actions, can never serve as a pretext for a believer to be indifferent about Christ's return or about his Real Presence that is given to us in the Eucharist and that is promised to us until the end of time.

Someone who thirsts for the truth of God present in Jesus Christ cannot be content with an experience, however spiritual and interior it may be. "Where have you put him?" This is the cry of faith, and it cannot stop at being a question. It is precisely the most demanding believers who will ask the Church to strengthen them in their faith in the reality of Christ's Resurrection. It is fortunate that we cannot explain the mode of this existence, because it is divine. But nothing ever requires us to content ourselves with a presence that has been reduced to a project, an idea, a word, an experience, or a memory.

For centuries people lived thinking that human life is above all a mystery of communion with what is real. Man's greatness was to commune with everything through knowledge and through love. But with the advent of mathematics and technology, at least three centuries ago, a revolution gradually took place. And, imperceptibly, it invaded everything. The human condition was no longer experienced primarily as a capacity for communion but rather as a productive or even creative force: the important thing was no longer to listen to reality but to manufacture it. And people marveled at this formidable creative power of man's mind. The problem was no longer to know whether one was arriving at what is true or false, but simply to fabricate, to produce. Man discovered himself as a new god, dazzled by the spontaneity and vitality of his own mind, inebriated with the discovery that he was the source, designer, and maker of his own living conditions. He took charge of himself. He created himself by creating; he discovered an infinite expanse within himself—this power of fabricating everything, even ideas. Then, little by little, people stopped attaching importance to error or truth. People learned to have nothing to do with anything that was not themselves. No more reality external to us, no more reality that could exist outside of us and resist us, to which we would still have to measure up, because from now on

we could build everything, master everything, modify everything, even the source of our thinking. . . .

   That is how we got to the point, as far as the faith is concerned, of living by proxy in a realm of diagrams and theories that had to be neat, pure, and transcendental, even at the
price of being nonexistent. Of course, everyday life remained,
with its fears, its conflicts, its hopes, playing itself out in the
realm of routine experience, of concrete things that still exist
and put up resistance. But it would be unfitting, they told us,
and "unworthy of God" to think that he could intervene in
that world. And we found ourselves subtly pressured to abandon, little by little, the conviction that there could be a reality beyond our ideas and our formulas. The faith was driven
back into an unsubstantial universe, without real contact with
anything outside of our thoughts or our desires. As Hegel put
it: "They nailed Christ to a cross of concepts."

   Gone were the days of a reality that surpassed us and that
could really be grasped despite the incompleteness of our formulas. Just as it would be too unworthy of God to compro-
mise himself and enter the universe that can be perceived by
our senses, it would be an illusion to attempt to make real contact with the historical Jesus. We would just have to get over
this habit of taking as real something that is only words, ideas,
or symbols: the Resurrection of Christ, his Real Presence in
the Eucharist, prayer, pardon, the hereafter. Those beliefs might
be useful in regulating social behavior, helpful ideas for those
who need to calm their anxiety or make history acceptable,
but all that would not exist as something real, real in the way
that it is real for a wife to meet again with her husband who
leaves the hospital cured after his life has been in danger; the
way that a birth is real, or the love of a father for his children.

   Intoxicated with creating and fabricating, we have developed a fear of a reality that we might no longer be able to

control, one that would not bend to our use as our ideas and plans do. We fear a reality that would no longer simply be our slave, like our technology and our devices; a reality that would put up resistance and would not let itself be rendered antiseptic or reduced to what we know about ourselves. We have fear of a reality that would exist independently of us, that would intervene in our world, our life, and our hopes—a reality whose coming would never allow the status quo to continue, just as after the Annunciation or the Crucifixion or the Resurrection things were never again the way they had been before. Similarly, after every meeting with Christ in the Gospel and after every true prayer, our life runs the risk of being profoundly changed.

Some people wish they could ask religion to deliver us all from the need to arrive at this reality we cannot master: "Isn't there a quick surgical procedure to remove this anxiety?" They would much prefer a God who would confine himself to the realm of ideas and remain vaporous, a God who would have nothing to do with everyday, empirical things, so that successive cultures could inexpensively refurbish the shifting image for themselves. They would just as soon have an antiseptic faith, from which all the salient reality had been amputated, so that there would be no more confrontation because no troublesome reality would be left.

"You run the risk", they tell us, "of reifying." That says it all: the main objection you hear in certain quarters: "Why do you speak about the Resurrection, the Real Presence in the Eucharist, or sin as though they were real things?" It is all quite consistent. A faith that ended up as a climate-controlled system of ideas, a set of abstractions that left nothing to fear or hope for, would no longer be of any interest. It would no longer be the faith.

The most formidable declaration of optimism we will ever encounter is rooted in an old intuition of Christian thought. It is the certainty that there is something in us that did not fall with Adam. And this something is the wondering apprehension of things, of being, of that which is beyond abstractions and which sin itself cannot obliterate: it is our taste for reality. Every person, whatever his anxieties, his psychological idiosyncrasies or imbalances, is nonetheless always capable, when he thinks, of reaching not only the more or less distorted world of his ideas, but reality itself. And the progress of every mind ends, not in the mirror of concepts, but in a state of rest in that which exists and resists. It is impossible to throw the human mechanism into complete disorder. Something will remain right. The Church has always said this: We are designed to be open to reality.

Out of a concern for liberating the faith, various voices have proclaimed the end of the era of discursive theology, of well-regulated systems of ideas, the end of metaphysics and of logocentrism. But when you come right down to it, what will free us most effectively from the oppression of theses and hypotheses and the power of the mandarins if not the Creed? With it, we know in what direction our thought is going, and, thanks to it, the faith of those who have precious little time or education can avoid doubts and useless detours. In the name of the faith, Saint Paul preached in Athens and opened the door of the golden cage in which the idols of thought imprisoned the human mind.

Faith: Humility and Transcendence

Archbishop Ryan does not hold up Ireland as a model. He has the humility to tell us that he is not at all sure that it still deserves the title of the "island of saints and scholars".

But the humility that he appeals to for the sake of the
faith goes deeper than that of a sociological view of his
Church. It is the humility of someone who knows that the
reality for which man was made is not just fabricated; rather,
it is received. We receive it from God. We receive it through
the Church in the Creed. We receive it on our knees, and
it transcends us. That is why we need all the wisdom of
our Fathers in faith, the wisdom of the memory of the
past. But it is not a question of the memory of a cultural
patrimony that would be concerned about consulting ecclesiastical commentaries. It is a question of *remembering the
acts of God*. And if that is something beyond us, then it
makes us that much greater. "The essential truths of the
faith cannot be grasped immediately." It is no accident that
our adherence to God is formulated in a "symbol" of faith.

Archbishop Ryan happily insists on the role of memory
in catechesis and on the essential position of the Apostles'
Creed as the structure for a catechism. That is not just a
counterbalancing movement that would bring us back to
what was one of the effective means of handing on the
faith in the generations that went before us. The Creed is
not one solution among others. It provides us with what
is essential, what all generations have received in order to
tell us about the creative and benevolent plan of God
(Eph 1). It allows us to minimize effort in the inquiries
and gropings of the human mind in search of meaning. It
spares those who have little sophistication or education
the trouble of retracing the laborious path of preceding
centuries and brings us instead promptly to certainties about
God. It proclaims the essentials of what has held and still
"holds together" all ages, all times, and all cultures of the
people consisting of the sons of God. Beyond all the commentaries and the rafts of scholarly works about the nature

of the Church, it tells us what *is*, in a simple, liberating affirmation.

"Symbol" means "what holds together". The etymology of the word is magnificent. It is itself an image. Among the Greeks, a symbol was a wooden object or a piece of pottery broken in two. The guest gave one half of it to his host and kept the other half. Each one bequeathed his part to his children, so that by bringing together their respective parts they themselves might be brought together in some way. A simple piece of wood or pottery thus became a force that could maintain relationships even over a great distance and could serve as a means of exchange, communication, and tradition. It was proof enough to recognize one another by.

We do precisely this in laying hold of the "symbol" of faith, that is, the Creed. It was given to us by our Fathers, handed down by the lessons of the past. We possess only one part of reality. We have to have that other part, the light that has come from God, in order to know ourselves. And so it is, thanks to this symbol, that we can recognize the reality of the mystery, the life of God to which we are invited. We used to live in a two-dimensional world. Through this symbol of faith, we enter into the three-dimensional world where true life is found. An image will serve to illustrate this reflection.

A painter stopped at a Japanese inn one evening to spend the night. After dinner, just before going to bed, he painted a cat at the bottom of the *fusama*, the sliding panel that closed the room. During the night a great noise of a chase broke out. At dawn, the painter left, and when the innkeeper went into the room, the cat that had been painted on the *fusama* the previous evening had disappeared, but nearby two mice lay dead on the *tatami* [straw mat].

It would be so easy for us if the divine guest were content to draw little figures on the panel of our life ... , but instead he comes as a thief in the night, and we do not know where he comes from or where he is going, and he causes chases and disturbances that we were not expecting. He is not content just to draw. To *know* God, to live with Christ, is to enter into a new order of existence. It is a question of the Life that is more than life. It is a question of the Glory of God who, from this moment on, invites, fascinates, and inflames us. And this really happens. The truths of faith cannot be reduced to antiseptic hypotheses. They are life, food, communion, the gift of conversion. They introduce us into a new order of life: one in which the acts of God become our acts, starting with the purification of our life ... , which sometimes leaves the mice of illusion on the *tatami*.

Nowadays courage means witnessing peaceably and joyfully to the inexhaustible light of the Creed. It is not just a matter of going from the dogmas to the faith, but also from the faith to the dogmas, which is to say, letting oneself be guided by these precise paths where every person is sure to encounter something other than the resonance of his illusions (disguised as ideas). It is true, this presupposes accepting the fact that we must beg tirelessly for light and admit that the formulas and presentations are always inadequate and unsatisfactory. But although words and concepts obviously cannot exhaust the mystery, this is no reason to deprive ourselves of this supreme mercy offered to our minds: knowing where to find the authentic plans that lead safely and surely to what is real. What sort of incarnational religion would it be that offered nothing but aspirin and tranquilizers to those who had survived the shipwreck of skepticism?

Godfried Cardinal Danneels

Archbishop of Malines-Brussels

Christian Faith and
the Wounds of Contemporary Man

Today, as in every age, the Lord unceasingly speaks to his people. For he loves them. He is a God of love and mercy. Here is what the Lord says through the mouth of his prophet:

> Why will you still be struck down,
>   that you continue to rebel?
> The whole head is sick,
>   and the whole heart faint.
> From the sole of the foot even to the head,
>   there is no soundness in it,
> but bruises and sores
>   and bleeding wounds;
> they are not pressed out, or bound up,
>   or softened with oil. . . .
> And the daughter of Zion is left
>   like a booth in a vineyard,
> like a lodge in a cucumber field,
>   like a besieged city." (Is 1:5–6, 8)

Conference held on January 22–23, 1983.

Yes, mankind and the Church at the end of this century—
that is to say, all of us—we are wounded. It hardly takes the
insight of a prophet to notice it. But the same Isaiah shows
us the therapy, the One who can heal all our ills.

> [The Servant of the Lord . . . ,] a man of sorrows, and
>   acquainted with grief;
> and as one from whom men hide their faces
>   he was despised, and we esteemed him not.
>
> Surely he has borne our griefs
>   and carried our sorrows. . . .
> But he was wounded for our transgressions,
>   he was bruised for our iniquities;
> upon him was the chastisement that made us whole,
>   and *with his stripes we are healed.* (Is 53:3–5)

Our century is wounded, perhaps more than any other period
in history. The fever affects not only the body: it is also a
fever of the mind and the soul. "The whole head is sick,
and the whole heart faint" (Is 1:5). More than ever our
world is seeking the "bronze serpent set on a pole" (cf. Num
21:9) so as to be rescued. More and more these days, Christianity is proving to be the only therapy capable of healing
man and contemporary society. Faith heals. Moreover, this
is the cry with which John Paul II inaugurated his pontificate:
"Do not be afraid to welcome Christ and accept his
power. . . . Do not be afraid. Open wide the doors for
Christ. . . . Do not be afraid. Christ knows 'what is in man'.
He alone knows it." [1]

---

[1] John Paul II, "Homily at the Mass of Installation Marking the Beginning of His Pastoral Ministry, Sunday, 22 October [1978]," *L'Osservatore romano,*
English edition, no. 44 (November 2, 1978): 12.

What Good Is the Christian Faith?

What good is the Christian faith? This is a question that dwells in the heart of many people, even though it does not always get as far as their lips. A large number of our contemporaries, especially in the West, have already answered this question: The faith is good for nothing. To be sure, it could be that this is not a definitive answer, but it is nonetheless clear. For many men and women of this century, the faith offers nothing that could satisfy their everyday needs. For Western man, in the great majority of cases, the Christian faith—or any religion at all—brings neither happiness nor the solution to our problems, healing for neither the body nor the heart.

And yet there is this very simple answer that a peasant woman gave to this question that was asked in a survey taken a few years ago: "Religion", she said, "is good for making you happy, or else it's good for nothing."

Believing is a source of happiness, and religion can be for mankind like being on an oxygen supply: profoundly therapeutic for culture and society.

I realize how abrupt and even daring this statement is. It will arouse opposition; for some people it could even cause new wounds. For in our age, what a lot of healers of body and soul there are! And how many quacks! The mistrust of contemporary man is understandable.

But I do not retract my statement. The healing of the entire man—body, heart, and soul—is part of the very core of Jesus' message.

> And he went about all Galilee, teaching in their synagogues and preaching the gospel of the kingdom and healing every disease and every infirmity among the people.... And they brought him all the sick, those afflicted with

> various diseases and pains, demoniacs, epileptics, and par-
> alytics, and he healed them. (Mt 4:23–24)

Obviously faith cannot be reduced to its therapeutic powers. It also introduces believers into the invisible world of
grace. But grace has its extensions into the realm of the
visible and the sensible. It is never foreign to the fortunes
of the human body. It can heal it now as in the days of the
early Church.

The relation between the Christian faith and the health
of mankind is a highly developed theme in contemporary
literature. The number of publications devoted to this subject keeps increasing. An author from the Netherlands, Han
Fortmann, writes:

> At the beginning of this century, the subject scarcely ever
> appeared in print; in 1945, one or two authors began to
> speak about it; nowadays there are innumerable publica-
> tions. Expressions like "mental health", "mental hygiene",
> and the entire psychotherapeutic terminology from now on
> are part of the average student's vocabulary.[2]

But is faith really as therapeutic as all that? Indeed, there is
no lack of evidence in human history that could suggest
the opposite. The heroes of faith and sanctity have not always
been models of psychological equilibrium. Just think of Sim-
eon Stylites, living for over forty-five years on a column in
the Syrian desert; of Francis of Assisi, who, driven by a
transport of irresistible love, kissed a leper at a time when
any contagion was fatal; of Philip Neri, who was not afraid
of ridicule; of Saint Benedict Joseph Labre—who died exactly
two centuries ago this year [that is, in 1683]—who was
certainly not a model of personal hygiene; of Charles de

---

[2] H. Fortmann, *Heel de mens*, p. 56.

Foucauld, walking through the streets of Nazareth, pursued by children who mocked him and threw stones at him. He considered it an honor to be able to suffer for Christ. Was he a masochist? Everyone knows that Saint Jerome, one of the great saints and scholars of Christian antiquity, was reputed to be one of the most difficult characters of his age; his letter to the young Augustine of Hippo, who had sent him one of his first treatises as a token of his esteem, dispels all doubts on this count. Then there is Thérèse of Lisieux, who at the age of thirteen had to struggle not to burst into tears because of a remark her father made (about her still receiving gifts) on Christmas Eve. Father Bruno, who for many years has been editor-in-chief of the journal *Études carmélitaines*, quotes the dreadful remark of Hildegard von Bingen: "God does not dwell in bodies that are well." Is there, then, something like an ecclesiogenic neurosis? Is sanctity built on the ruins of sanity and physical health? And let no one say that the superiors are to blame for this state of affairs because of their severity. Often it is the candidate for sainthood himself who has to be stopped along the rough road of asceticism. For the self-denial of which the Gospel speaks cannot mean a mutilation of the person; it is a transcendence of self through love and joy. And in order to transcend oneself, one must first calmly accept oneself.

Even if, over the course of the history of Christian holiness, certain saints traveled the rugged roads of an exaggerated corporeal austerity, the great tradition of Christian sanctity did not go that route. The joy that impregnates the account of creation from the very first page of the Bible and the stream of optimism that runs through the entire Bible lead to Jesus, who heals the paralytic at the same time that he pardons his sins: healing and the forgiveness of sins

are two sides of the same reality (cf. Mt 9:1–8). Furthermore the Latin term *salus* means healing, well-being, safety;
and the Germanic root *Heil* is the basis for the adjective
"whole", in the sense of "entire, sound, complete". Faith
completes man down to the innermost fibers and the most
hidden areas of his being. It restores to man his perfection;
it makes him truly himself. In the First Letter to the Corin-
thians, Paul writes these surprising lines: "For any one who
eats and drinks without discerning the body [of Christ] eats
and drinks judgment upon himself. That is why many of
you are weak and ill, and some have died" (1 Cor 11:29–
30). Of course, this passage must be interpreted, but not to
the point where it is made to say exactly the opposite of its
literal meaning. Moreover, in many prayers after communion, the Church does not hesitate to ask for "the healing
of body and soul through this communion with the Body
and the Blood of the Lord". Finally, healing and sacrament
are inseparable in the theology of the anointing of the sick
as well as in its liturgical celebration. The latter, indeed,
refers to the famous passage from the Letter of James: "Is
any among you sick? Let him call for the elders of the
Church, and let them pray over him, anointing him with
oil in the name of the Lord; and the prayer of faith will
save the sick man, and the Lord will raise him up; and if he
has committed sins, he will be forgiven" (Jas 5:14–15). Is
this something obsolete? A regression? Or a reality hidden
and passed over in silence by a theological rationalism?

Let us conclude with an impartial witness, Gustav Jung.
He writes:

> When one of my patients is a practicing Catholic, without
> exception I advise him to go to confession and commu-
> nion.... For the Protestants it is not that easy, since their

doctrine and worship have become so pale that to a great extent they have lost their efficacy. I am absolutely convinced that a large number of people should be members of the Catholic Church, because they would really feel at home there.

Of course, Jung is not infallible, and he keeps strictly to the therapeutic and pragmatic level. Moreover he refuses to state an opinion about the theological truth of Catholicism. It is the simple observation of a great psychologist. Let us conclude, therefore, that it is wrong to say that all dogma leads to dogmatism and all rites lead to ritualism. Dogma and ritual can be deeply therapeutic for the man who is trying to find his bearings in a ruined world. Moreover, this is true also on the level of civilization, culture, and society.

A New Neurosis?

The Dutch psychiatrist J. Van den Berg writes,

It is almost certain that neurotic disturbances were rarely encountered in Europe before the eighteenth century. Before 1733, there is no book on medicine that mentions neuroses. Now, if there had been any, the average physician could easily have established their existence. Even an unqualified layman would have had no difficulty in noticing them. But we find no trace of them. Certainly, there was no lack of complicated or bizarre personalities. The character of Hamlet in Shakespeare's play and some of Molière's characters exhibit great complexity. But a person whose character and psychological profile are relatively complicated is not, for all that, a neurotic.

From that period on, the situation has reversed itself. Neuroses and psychological illnesses are invading our society like

an epidemic; everybody talks about them; providing medical treatment for them has become a major task for our
Western society.

Something has changed, therefore. But what? Here is one
hypothesis. I have borrowed it from the same Doctor Van
den Berg. Before the eighteenth century, the typical European lived in a harmonious universe; he was situated within
a network of well-integrated relationships. His relation with
God, with the universe, with the cosmos, his relationships
with other men, with society, and with himself were well
defined. Everything had its place, and there was a place for
everything. There was a firmly established frame of reference, and religion was the cement holding it together. The
rules of the game in religion—if we can put it that way—in
morality and in politics were clearly determined and generally accepted.

From the eighteenth century on, however, things changed.
Many authors speak of a "repression of sexuality and aggressiveness" in modern man. Hence the beginning of a considerable number of neuroses, which were later identified
by psychoanalysis. And that, they say, is the source of the
sadness that weighs down the Western world.

There is no denying that this repression was the cause of
a certain number of neuroses in Western man. Studies and
clinical practice by what is called psychoanalysis have con-
tributed much to healing the afflicted, and they will continue to do so. No one would deny the importance of this
work of integrating vital impulses in the consciousness, so
that they serve the flourishing of the person.

But since then, sexuality and aggressiveness have made a
spectacular comeback: what was until very recently the object
of an unconscious repression has metamorphosed into a ver-
itable "sustenance", a universal requirement. Sexuality has

lost its mystery to become eroticism, which is often commercialized. Aggressiveness leads to violence that blinds and destroys, often without any apparent motive. The two sisters who were once exiled have returned as accomplices, and now they are everywhere. *Des Guten zuviel!* [Too much of a good thing.]

Now, if sexuality and aggression are no longer banished from consciousness, if they are no longer repressed, and therefore if this apparent cause of our neuroses is gone, why do we still not feel well? For no one would say that contemporary Western man is happy. Of course, there is the economic crisis, which is real, and then there are the illnesses that keep reappearing in new forms, despite medical progress. But is there not something else? Why are Westerners who are well and find themselves in rather comfortable living conditions so "vaguely unhappy"? All of Western civilization is blanketed with the light and almost smiling mist of melancholy. So the neurosis is still there; it remains! Man's sexual liberation and unbridled aggression are no cure. Why not? What is the cause of the discreet and civilized suffering of contemporary man?

Here is Van den Berg's hypothesis. We have "repressed" another component of our human existence, driving it out of the consciousness into the subconscious. As was the case with sexuality and aggressiveness, we have repressed the sense of God and of the transcendent. What sort of silence surrounds God in our age? In the daily routine, at table, in the workplace, in society, in a word, wherever man lives out his important decisions, no one ever speaks about God. The entire realm of religion, faith, and God, the domain of "spirituality", is banished from everyday life and marginalized. The problem of the fall and redemption, of life and death: Who cares?

Now it is the whole spiritual side that has been repressed. The result is the same: a new neurosis, the main symptom of which is silence about God. That, then, is our deep wound. Contemporary man represses this sense of the transcendent which is precisely what makes him human. For an essential part of man is his relation to God. As Pascal put it, man infinitely surpasses man. An atheistic humanism, as noble as it might be, will never be able to grasp all the riches of man. In such a world view, man is like "the torso of a Greek sculpture, headless, without arms or legs, a divine fragment that sings the hymn of pure form" (Théophile Gauthier). He resembles those half-finished statues of Michelangelo that yearn to emerge from the marble and be set free. Such is man without God: he is incomprehensible in his profound abundance. Some of our contemporaries sense this: in the midst of the crisis of meaning they glimpse the dawn. After all, André Malraux remarked that the twenty-first century will be a metaphysical and religious century. Might that not be the neurosis of our age: this conspiracy of silence about God? If we want to be cured, will we not have to start pronouncing God's name aloud again, speaking about him and giving him thanks?

We are all suffering in this domain of spirituality, and we all bear the marks of it. Someone who suffers in this way is not physically sick. But he has a deficiency in simple joy: he is "vaguely sad". The new neurosis is spiritual. That is what has to be cured.

"When the Father Is Gone, the Children Are Cold"

The fundamental reality that Jesus came to reveal to mankind is that of the paternity of God, of a God of love who is Father. Even the Old Testament speaks about God as a

Father: the Father of the people, of the king, of the just. But it nevertheless remains true that this revelation of the Father is the special mission of Jesus and constitutes the very heart of the New Testament. The first Christian writers have preserved the expression "Abba-Father" as they received it from the lips of Jesus; they did not consider it necessary to translate it. Even Saint Paul, who never knew Christ in the flesh, has recorded this expression, so characteristic it was of Jesus (Rom 8:15; Gal 4:6).

Psychological studies have shown us the structure and the essential character of the bond with the father in human development; they have also described its pathological states. Man, indeed, is often wounded and scarred in this respect. It is not easy nowadays for a child to reach adulthood having established a liberating and fulfilling relationship with his father. Moreover this is just as true for the development of mankind as a whole. Since the beginning of the modern era, man's relationship to God, the Father of mankind, has suffered violence. And the filial dependence upon God that is experienced through religion has been vilified as a pathological regression. It is undeniable that religion, too, is no stranger to pathology: a Father-God can overwhelm the sons. Man turns then to rebellion; he would like to free himself from the oppressive tie that binds him to a divine oppressor. For those who are weaker, religion turns into anxiety. Nietzsche experienced this tragedy. He came to the conclusion that if mankind is to attain adulthood, this necessarily implies the death of God. Ever since then, the death of God has been a classical theme in the Western world.

The era in which we live has largely eliminated God from cultural, intellectual, and social life. Entire generations have fought the very idea of God's existence. This was the cost of man's flourishing and the progress of civilization. There is no room for two kings of the universe: God and man. So the curtain on heaven was closed, all the holes in the firmament were plugged, and the back of the stage set was forgotten. God was dead; now man could be born. From now on the path leading to happiness was ahead of us, wide open.

But has all that come true since then? Has man really become more fulfilled, happier, more human, after that long period of imposed or freely chosen atheism?

On the contrary, man has lost has soul; the world has grown cold. "When the Father is gone, the children are cold." When God disappears, people look for other sources of warmth. But where are they to be found? For the Father is no more, and we are all orphans. Here is a prophetic text. It is taken from the book *The Raw Youth* by Dostoyevsky, written almost 150 years ago, at the dawn of this era of atheistic humanism:

> If men were to become orphans, they would stand by one another more closely and more affectionately; they would take each other's hands, understanding that henceforth they are entirely dependent on one another. Then the grandiose idea of immortality would disappear, and we would have to replace it; this extravagant love for the One who was immortality would be directed instead toward nature, the world, mankind, every blade of grass. . . . They would awaken and hurry to embrace each other; they would hasten to love, knowing that their days were passing quickly and that that is all they had left. They would work for each other, and each one would give everything to everyone and thus would be happy. Every child would know and feel that every person on earth is a father and a mother to him.

Yes, when the father is gone, the children shiver from the cold. "Just let God go away", they said, and here we are now in the middle of winter. Our whole civilization is as though frozen over; love, too. Contacts among races and languages have ossified; there is so little solidarity, so little warmth in society; there is nothing but the dull, metallic sound of conflict or the silence of mistrust. We are all like birds in winter. While waiting, we gather around the rare sources of heat, the last remaining places in our civilization where there are still a few glowing coals under the ashes: namely, love and festivity, which are often pushed to the extremes of erotic fever or orgy. But all of that does not bring back the warmth. The fires have been extinguished, both literally and figuratively. Where is the sun, then? Where is God? For without him any fire is nothing but a straw fire that lasts only a moment and cannot really warm the children.

When the sun disappears, man changes. All our relationships change, even those that connect us with nature: the plants and the animals suddenly become the object of a boundless ecological devotion. We try to restore Mother Nature. Cruelly exploited at first, she now receives a semblance of order from our efforts. It is like a Japanese garden: two cherry trees, three pebbles in a pool of water and the reassuring noise of a fountain somewhere. But all that does not warm us or heal our loneliness.

We have to find something else. Yes, we must rediscover childhood and our filial relationship with the Father. And it is possible. From this Promethean self-affirmation at the dawn of the adulthood of our civilization, a second naïveté can emerge, a recovery of spontaneity. This second childhood will not be identical to the first one, because it will have passed the age of critical reason. It will be different. But it will find again the joy and simplicity of childhood, enriched this time with the fruits of suffering.

Jesus said, "Unless you ... *become* like children, you will never enter the kingdom of heaven" (Mt 18:3). True childhood, therefore, is ahead of us; we must ask for it and receive it as a grace. This is what can cure us: the recovered sense of our divine sonship, entering into a second childhood, the passage from knowledge to wisdom, from the head to the heart.

To rediscover God as a Father and to enter with Christ into that filial experience: that is the Christian faith, and it is profoundly therapeutic for our civilization. In the West, the untrammeled growth of the self has developed into cancer. In this crisis, mankind has lost its sense of God, and by that very fact man has lost his identity and his joy. For every attack leveled at God wounds human nature deeply. It saddens.

The passage by Dostoyevsky is prophetic in another respect, also. It seems to suggest that the absence of our common Father is betrayed by a frantic search for fraternity and cohesiveness among the orphaned children. The disappearance of the vertical dimension ultimately leads to an exaltation of horizontal relationships. The warmth of the sun must be replaced by the warmth of the nest. Indeed, since God's disappearance, we have never witnessed such a search for communication, solidarity, societal engineering, and world planning as we see today. The "we" swallows up the "me" under the pretext of saving or protecting it. This feverish search for all sorts of communities, large and small—could it have anything to do with the obliteration of the Father? Is universal brotherhood possible in the absence of a common Father? The ignorance of the Father obliges men to prove to each other that they belong to the same family. And they have to provide this proof over and over, at every moment.

Being Accepted as One Is—Love and Mercy

This is the heart of the Gospel message, and the secret of healing. As the Apostle John says in his first letter: "In this is love, not that we loved God but that he loved us and sent his Son to be the expiation for our sins" (1 Jn 4:10). By becoming man, God accepted us as we are, with our history of falling and getting up again. We do not have to stand on tiptoe in order to merit God's love. He does not consider our talents, our qualities, or even our good will before he loves us: He loves us gratuitously. He weds poor mankind by saying to each one of us, "I wish to take you as my bride; I promise to honor and love you, in good times and in bad; I want to love you for all eternity." Through the Incarnation, this source of healing for mankind is manifested: God accepts us as we are so as to be able to love us forever.

God accepts us as we are. This is what can cure us. Our era is characterized by a tremendous lack of acceptance. "O that you would tear the heavens and come down" (Is 64:1). This cry that the people in darkness address to God: every husband repeats it to his wife, every wife to her husband, every child to his father and mother, every parent to his child. To be accepted and to accept the other, is that not the most important form of therapy for our era?

To accept one's fellowman who lives under the same roof— when two people begin to live together, one might think: my fellowman is like me, he is my image, a second me, another self. He resembles me in everything; he thinks as I do and feels as I do. But everything changes so quickly. My fellowman is different: he is quite unlike me; he is a little bit like God. He asks me to accept him as he is. He says to me, "O, if you could only tear your heavens in two and come down to me. Take me as I am, accept me; do not make me stand always on tiptoe, trying to please you. For I am different."

No one is more astonishingly different than a child. He is the offspring of the couple, but he is quite different. For a while at first, the child, too, is like a second self in the eyes of his parents, their perfect image. But day by day the child reveals himself to be quite different, and his demand becomes more and more urgent: "Take me, then, as I am. Love me, not because I resemble you, but for what I am. Bring me into this world a second time. For there is a twofold paternity and maternity and a twofold birth." The first time, the man and the woman claim as their own the biblical verse, "I have begotten my likeness with the help of the Lord" (cf. Gen 4:1). They love their child because of that resemblance. But there is a second fatherhood and motherhood: the one that accepts the child for his own sake, as he is, different and unique. Every child is begotten a second time when his parents accept him in his other-ness. This child, who is nonetheless flesh of our flesh and blood of our blood, is so different from us. Thousands of families live this paradox in suffering. The child says to his parents, "You have given me life the first time; now become my father and my mother a second time. For I am different." And conversely, thousands of parents say to their children: "No doubt we are not as you would have wished. We are different, too; we have grown older, we are different. Take us as we are and become our children a second time."

Then there is the child who has no voice. The infant who is not yet born and is incapable of defending himself. Yet he is there, he has been announced, although perhaps unexpectedly. He is so silent. But he cries out all the louder:

"Accept me. Give me a name. Take me as I am. I am your child."

Finally there are the strangers in our cities. They, too, unceasingly cry out to us: "O, if you could only tear your heavens in two so as to come down to us! Accept us as we are!"

In a world that suffers so much lack of acceptance, reconciliation, and love, the Christian faith can be profoundly therapeutic. It alone can restore a civilization of love modeled on the love with which God loves us. This love of God is realistic: it is not based on the qualities of the person loved; he loves him gratuitously, creating for himself the qualities he would like to see in the beloved. Certainly, the Gospel tells us, "Be perfect, as your heavenly Father is perfect" [Mt 5:48]; and "when you have done all that is commanded you, say, 'We are unworthy servants'" [Lk 17:10]. He is making radical demands, then. But it is nonetheless true that whatever God demands of us, he begins to give us as a gift. He *commands*, and he *gives*. He does even more: he *forgives*, if we do not respond to his demands. God alone is capable of combining these three things: commanding, giving, and forgiving [*ordonner, donner, pardonner*]. For any other authority figure, that would be self-destructive. That is the power of love in God, the Love who is God: he accepts us as we are, long before we are aware of it and long after we have fled far from him. For "in this love consists: not that we have loved God but that he loved us [first] and sent his Son to be the expiation for our sins" (cf. 1 Jn 4:10). And again: "My little children, I am writing this to you so that you may not sin; but if any one does sin, we have an advocate with the Father, Jesus Christ the righteous; and he is the expiation for our sins, and not for ours only but also for the sins of the whole world" (1 Jn 2:1–2).

"The Truth Will Make You Free."

Contemporary man is wounded in a way of which he is scarcely conscious: he suffers from the crisis in truth. For centuries now philosophical systems and ideologies have come and gone in an uninterrupted series, and the net effect has been to immerse contemporary man in skepticism and perplexity. "Where is truth?" Pilate's question has become ours, the question of an entire civilization. The very search for truth has been abandoned; the seeker is weary, tired of the pursuit. Man needs a true message, a place at which to anchor. For our problem is not just the cold; it is the darkness, too. Sure, we are cold, and that is why we are looking for the last fires that have remained lit on this earth. But what good is it to be warm, if you are in the dark? Love is not enough; we need also, and first of all, the truth, without which the fire is nothing but a straw fire. At the heart of the Christian message is inscribed this psalm verse which is chanted in the Christmas liturgy: "Kindness and truth shall embrace" (cf. Ps 85:11 NAB). That is why we must return to the simplicity of the Gospel and of tradition, to the sources of the message as it was revealed by the prophets and the apostles, as it is preached in the Church.

Where do our wounds come from? Why our lack of joy? The Gospel that Francis of Assisi had was no different from ours. Why, then, was he so much more joyful than we are? Because Francis adhered to the Gospel as it is: *Evangelium sine glossa*, the Gospel without additives. While reading the Gospel, Francis left the margins blank and wrote no annotations: the Gospel without revisions or, as he puts it, the text undiluted by commentary. Then the Word of God, sharp as an arrow, strikes the listener right in the heart. It causes many wounds, but they heal quickly and well. Let us not write between the lines, for then we prevent the Word of God from healing us. We deprive it of its therapeutic value.

This is not to say that there cannot be explanations or commentaries on the Gospel. They are quite helpful to us and bring us light and understanding. But will joy spring from that? What is its source, if not first and foremost the simple obedience of faith, rendered with the heart of a child? Perhaps Francis was often mistaken with regard to "scientific" exegesis, but he made no mistake about the deeper meaning of Scripture, because he had a heart that was obedient and perfectly free. That is why he instantly understood what God wanted to tell him. But there is more. Francis always remained within the bosom of the Church's living tradition. There, in the midst of the waters of that great river, he received that message. "No one showed me what I ought to do", he wrote in his testament. "But the Most High himself revealed to me that I should live according to the Holy Gospel. I had [the Rule] written down in a few very simple words, and the good Pope approved it for me."

We can understand the Word of God only by placing ourselves within the great current of the Church's living tradition; that is where we find all those great ones and lowly ones, the saints and the sinners, the scholars and the unlettered, the pastors and the little people, all those who have listened. The Word of God is comprehensible only for someone who receives it in the Church's maternal bosom. That is where it can be conceived, carried, and nourished, where it can be protected and continually restored to its equilibrium. Like a child in his mother's womb. . . .

Leave Everything to Receive a Hundredfold

There are other reasons for this absence of joy in contemporary man. It results also from the fact that we so rarely say Yes to the Word of God, in whatever form it presents itself. The initial Yes, that of humble listening, is a source of joy, of Marian joy. Now, our hearts are often so sad because our Yes is immediately followed by a "but" that revises it. This "but" is like the stone that just seals off the source of joy. This "yes, but" always saddens profoundly. Do we see why?

Man is like a tree. God planted it in the garden of his creation, staked it firmly in the earth, rooted it three times. Our roots are the innate desire for ownership, sexuality, and self-fulfillment. So it is that God created us, as we read on the first page of the Bible. With the comment: "And God saw that it was good." But our tree is like the castor-oil plant belonging to the prophet Jonah: there is a little worm gnawing at its roots. Jonah's plant had sprouted overnight; it was quite firm and sound; the next night it was dried up. It is the same with us: the desire for money, to start a family, to have children, to be fulfilled: that is the firm, green tree that is sound. But everything can change overnight. Why does the desire to have things so quickly become a passion that is taken to extremes? This uncontrolled rush after money, sex, and self-aggrandizement is just lethal. What was good in and of itself, a sign of health, becomes pathological. Good cells multiply unchecked: that is cancer. Sorrow comes along with it: what was supposed to make man happy plunges him into sadness. Many of our sullen moods result from this: we are fettered to so many things, to the point of having lost that complete freedom of paradise. The old man has taken up residence in us. Here is the reason for our lack of joy: the tree is good, the roots, too. But . . . there is that worm. . . .

Yet at the same time, we cannot help being moved by the radicalism of the Gospel. It is stronger than we are:

> Truly, I say to you, there is no one who has left house or brothers or sisters or mother or father or children or lands, for my sake and for the gospel, who will not receive a hundredfold now in this time, houses and brothers and sisters and mothers and children and lands, with persecutions, and in the age to come eternal life. (Mk 10:29–30)

For "the old man" cannot stifle that other latent but strong desire within us to become a "new man", begotten by the Spirit. That is why there will always be some people who march to a different drummer: the poor, the chaste, and the obedient. They have abandoned everything so as to receive everything in return, and a hundredfold. Behold, in our own days, the desert is being repopulated by a new people and is flourishing. They discover there another joy.

In our best moments, we cannot help seeking God, like the compass that points North. Our souls have been signed, and "God has set his eye upon [our] hearts" (cf. Sir 17:8). For even beyond our freedom, we are imbued with a profound desire for God: the image tends toward the One who made it, and all our interior paths lead to him. "For you formed my inward parts, you knitted me together in my mother's womb. . . . You know me right well" (Ps 139:13–14).

But there is more. Beyond all our attachments to riches, we possess, in the deepest part of ourselves, a taste for moderation and poverty. Beyond aggressiveness and violence, we conceal within ourselves an immense tenderness for all men, for all living things. However exuberant or careless we may be, all of us are overcome in certain hours by this sadness: Love himself is so little loved. And however dull our eye may be, it still has a nostalgia for purity and transparency. No doubt the Beatitudes are not the first things on our wish-list, but nevertheless they constitute our second nature, which grace has been bringing to birth in all mankind ever since Christ rose from the dead. We need only recall this language of the Beatitudes, and our hearts resonate to the last fiber. For that is how we are made: we were created in order to find God.

Like Elisha

There are many other wounds besides the ones I have just listed: think of the problems of disarmament and peace, hunger, the lack of freedom, oppression, human rights being scoffed at in so many places in the world. I have not spoken about these, and I beg your pardon. But doubtless others have done so. In those areas, too, the Christian faith heals. For my part, I wanted to look at the wounds in man's heart, from which comes all that is good and all that is evil. I wanted to speak with you this evening about interior healing.

For the Christian message, proclaimed in Scripture, collected and handed on by tradition, preached by the Church, is the power of resurrection for a world that is in agony. What is keeping us, then, from doing what Elisha did: "Then he went up and lay upon the child, putting his mouth upon his mouth, his eyes upon his eyes, and his hands upon his hands; and as he stretched himself upon him, the flesh of the child became warm ... and [he] opened his eyes. [He said to the mother:] 'Take up your son'" (2 Kings 4:34–36).

O Church,
Bride of Christ!
Make praise and thanks ascend
to the Son who gave you the Blood
by which you and your children
are healed each day!
(Liturgy of the Eastern Syrian Church)

Reflection by Georges Bonnet

The conference given by Godfried Cardinal Danneels addresses a question that has confronted Christians from the earliest days of the Church and that each cultural change raises again with new emphases in a different context: Does not the Christian faith denigrate man's efforts and yearnings with its suspicions and denunciations, to the point of separating man from himself and ruining him? This is not a new debate. It is not a secondary issue. It is terribly relevant. Far from mitigating the controversy, the presence of the Christian community in this world—already of long duration, with its vicissitudes and difficulties—has made it louder and more bitter.

Today the denial is taking a radical form. The conference speaker reports the peremptory declaration of certain voices that "Faith is good for nothing." Instead of providing answers to the questions that people ask themselves, it muddles the way in which they are expressed, disparaging certain desires. One would have to agree to lose oneself in order to be safe! This saying is perceived as hostile, disdainful, judgmental. Man must be solely his own. Completely. They have been saying it for ages: "Man is the measure of all things", and the Enlightenment philosophy has convinced the West of the human capacity for building a world of clarity, reason, and justice. Everything is possible for man. Discoveries, technological advances, abundance have followed, but also, unexpectedly, disillusionment and skepticism.

The results are not in keeping with the promises. The supposed mastery ultimately leads to a radical doubt, rigorously argued. Reason boasts of the suspicions that it has about everything and about itself. It analyzes and describes, careful to find the right words for its torment and its despair, the inconstancy of all things. Although the intellectual may revel in these high-flown, garrulous critiques, the ordinary working man finds them profoundly unsettling. He thinks that he has lost everything, like Job, relegated to a dunghill, scraping his sores with a pottery shard—but a Job without faith.

To this anxiety that crushes some people, to this torment that others embellish with a discreet charm (a sign of their independence and intelligence), the Christian message is not a tranquilizer with a temporary and superficial effect. It is a remedy. It heals.

Cardinal Danneels does not neglect to mention in this regard the possible detours and setbacks. Certain minds that equate serious thought with excess, paying little attention to complexity and the quality of things, have exhibited their intention to be faithful to the letter of the Scriptures by some very extravagant behaviors. This desire, indeed, can go astray even when it comes to prayer and asceticism. Nowadays we are better informed about the unconscious impulses that cause troubles and disorders when they are unduly acted out. But these deviations are not the faith. They do not spring from its tenets. Quite the contrary; they contradict its most essential truth, the one that insists on the Incarnation of the Lord, on his presence in everyday life, in the commonplace concerns of work and human relationships. They forget the man Jesus, the son of Mary, the carpenter of Nazareth, the one who saved us by being man perfectly—he who is the only begotten Son of God, the Creator of worlds and of spirits.

This diagnosis allows Cardinal Danneels to highlight two fundamental affirmations of the Christian faith that are often presented separately, without any organic connection, which distorts their meaning and weakens the proclamation of them: the creation account and the saving work of Jesus the Christ. Actually it is the dynamic continuity between them that manifests more vividly their salvific power, fulfilling man's deepest desire in a way surpassing anything he could express or wish.

Both of these realities are part of the economy of salvation, the unique plan of God the Savior. They should be proclaimed as closely related truths. Jesus the Christ is "the first-born of all creatures". In him and through him all things were made, in the Word that is at the same time Love and Reason, intelligence and self-gift. He is also "the first-born from among the dead", having been faithful to the truth about man even unto death on the Cross, thereby causing his own humanity to enter into the Glory of God.

But these two relations [of Christ as "first-born"] are "givens"—works of generosity, acts of love—and so they must be freely accepted. Each individual must consent to them in order to be himself in his ultimate truth, that is, to be a son of God in the One Son.

Indeed, every man "desires to be God". Sartre admits it, dramatically portraying the disturbance that such an aim causes. This aspiration has left its mark on civilizations and cultures. It renders them dynamic. Consequently, how can man avoid being torn, if he does not have what he most intensely desires, if he denies the one whom he would like to be?

The current disorder and disarray are the result of this. To reject God is to reject oneself, to deny the love that is at the origin of each one of us, whereas it is thought that we are rejecting the one who constantly finds fault with man, judges him strictly, and keeps him at a distance, ordering him around and imposing his stern sovereignty.

From a false notion of this relationship spring trouble and anxiety and even rebellion. Man refuses to consent to what he is: totally dependent on the One who gives existence to every creature. With the help of the imagination, the Creator is pictured with the characteristics of a distant potentate, demanding, inscrutable, and cold; modern man fears the Judge; he rejects this external Witness to whom he owes everything, including the ability to decide freely and to deny him. Summoning erudition and Freudian analyses, contemporary man strives to free minds from the phantasms and symbols that obsess and mutilate them. By hiding God behind a mask and then rejecting him, man finds himself not only orphaned but also deprived of himself, without identity, without bearings, delivered over to the randomness and caprice of the world, to the objects that he makes, to the senselessness of the passing days.

Christian revelation, as Godfried Cardinal Danneels reminds us, proclaims in this regard essential, fundamental truths that are liberating for man. By virtue of Creation, there is within man a capacity for what is divine. The Incarnation of the Word of God proves and manifests this. If man, in Jesus the Christ, is God himself present in humanity, it is because man, having issued from creative love, is "capable of divinity". He was deliberately willed for this grace and glory. Even when he is marked by limitation and evil, he is loved infinitely by God just as he is, because man, as he is, was created in the image and likeness of God.

That is to say that the Creator is neither opposed to nor at a distance from the one whom he brings into being. He thinks of him and wills him in a completely disinterested, gratuitous love, without reservation or mistrust. Man is tempted to picture this unparalleled act in terms that come from his own manner of being with others in spite of difficulties in communication, of living together with the attendant risks of resentment, envy, and jealousy.

Man can go astray and be lost. He has been given to himself, in complete freedom, to the point of being able to refuse his Maker. He can want to be himself, by himself, with nothing more, rejecting the profound relationship that joins him to the One who, by sheer goodness, gives him existence and sustains him in that infinite love.

Revelation purifies our spontaneous, distrustful, fearful way of coming to know God by disclosing the reason for his creative work, that is, by unveiling that which is beyond all reason: a Love that seeks love.

The second relation [of Christ as "first-born"], which is coordinated with the first, accomplishing the plan of creation, is the work of Christ the Savior, of the Crucified and Risen One. This God whom they want to ignore, whom they declare to be dead, was in fact ignored and put to death. But in this apparent obliteration and condemnation were realized the perfect presence of the God-man in the world of men and his unfailing fidelity to everything that man does, in his purity, his grandeur, and his capacity for good. Over Christ Jesus, who had lived out his life using the ordinary means of a man without power or wealth, death could not be victorious. Instead of having the last word, it enabled the one who suffered it to surpass that fatal limit in all justice and goodness and to enter bodily into the divine Glory.

To recognize the Savior in a condemned man; to have the daring and courage to look upon him taken down from the Cross after he underwent bodily death and was laid in a tomb.... Dostoyevsky, whose prophetic words Cardinal Danneels recalls, had been fascinated by the *Dead Christ* by Hans Holbein the Younger, which is displayed at the museum in Basel, Switzerland. Having climbed on a chair so as to have a better view of this astonishing painting, he was as though petrified. He murmured: "This canvas could make a believer lose his faith." Later on, however, he remarked in the notebooks for *The Brothers Karamazov*, "Oh, the crucifixion! It is a terrifying theme."

God, indeed, was not content with words alone. He is not aloof, distant from the world of men; rather, he is so given over to this world as to become its victim. Beyond the scandal caused by this body taken down from the Cross, the Christian discerns the one who utters God and man in that silent, torn, and peaceful moment preceding the glorious Resurrection.

Wounded man—the man of our time, we ourselves—in a world that no longer knows, despite its accumulation of scientific knowledge, that no longer wills, despite its plans and enterprises, and that categorically rejects the gospel message: this wounded man is not only the victim of himself and of his prideful excess. He is wounded also because he lived and fought in a fierce battle. Some of these wounds come from having served man, from having run up against the enigma of this world, from having experienced its constraints and rigors. His honor is that he took the risk, to the point that he was bruised by them. These wounds of the combatant do him justice, in contrast to those that never heal over but are always reopened by egotism and self-love.

May this wounded man look to the man on Calvary, marked with five wounds, the final and indelible records of his decisive action on behalf of man, sorrowful tokens of his battle against death. Risen now, he bears the marks forever. He showed them to unbelieving Thomas so that he might touch them and find that they are real and so that he might discover in those scars the proof of Life restored, the strength of Salvation.

> *"He has carried our sorrows . . .*
> *with his stripes we are healed."*
>   (Is 53:1–5)

Franciszek Cardinal Macharski

Archbishop of Krakow

Communicating the Faith
and the Test of Faith

My dear Friends,

1. The test of faith is the fight for freedom

In one of the last poems that Karol Cardinal Wojtyla wrote
in Krakow, we read:

Freedom has continually to be won,
it cannot merely be possessed.
It comes as a gift but can only be kept with a struggle. . . .
You pay for freedom with all your being,
therefore call this your freedom,
that paying for it continually you possess yourself anew. . . .

We must not consent to weakness.
Weak is a people that accepts defeat,
forgetting that it was sent
to keep watch
till the coming of its hour.
And the hours keep returning
on the great clock face of history.[1]

Conference held on January 29–30, 1983.

[1] "Thinking My Country," in *The Place Within: The Poetry of Pope John Paul
II*, trans. Jerzy Peterkiewicz (New York: Random House, 1982) pp. 145, 149.

The test of faith is the fight for freedom: yes, it is the fight for freedom with respect to God and, through him, for freedom with respect to man; it is the fight for freedom with respect to eternity and transcendence: from this freedom comes the freedom for everyday living. The test of faith is a spiritual event, from which man should emerge with an even greater freedom.

2. *The hour of testing is the hour of night*

Unceasingly in the history of salvation, the hour of trial strikes, in which the faith of the people of God is tested—for individuals and in a certain sense for communities. God, indeed, is always ready to give himself to each new generation: this is the essential message of the divine revelation definitively accomplished in Jesus Christ. Down through the centuries, therefore, and in the recesses of men's consciences, God's call—Come!—and his question—"Will you also go away?" (Jn 6:67)—continue to resound.

These hours of trial strike throughout the history of salvation, and by all indications they will not cease to strike, just as their repercussions are being felt now by persons and nations. . . . With what reverence we pronounce the names of our Fathers in faith, whose trials merited faith for us: Abraham, Isaac, Jacob, Moses—and that very precious name that is above all other names: that of Jesus, and of Mary, his Mother.

To us, who are experiencing the present time as a night, it appears that the hour of trial is precisely the hour of night: the night of the patriarch Jacob beside the stream of Jabbok; the night of Jesus, both in Gethsemane and on Golgotha; the night of John of the Cross, and how could we fail to mention: the night of Pascal. . . .

3. *May this hour be like the dawn of the resurrection*

My dear Friends, I tell you this as a pastor, concerned *about you*; and as a Christian concerned *together with you* about salvation: Will he find any faith in our generation? What will we hand down to the generation to come? The particular object of this concern is *this decisive point: the testing of our faith*. We want to help people—from their birth until their death—by using all possible means of communicating the faith within the Church, so that each one might find his place in the response of faith that the Church gives and so that each one might give his response.

This concern applies especially to those people and those spiritual arenas in which the drama of the trial is being played out. *How can we help them*, so that, after the night of wrestling (and agony), it will not be the cockcrow announcing the morning hour, but that hour will be instead like the dawn of the Resurrection and the hour of Pentecost. . . .

We do not proclaim a Christianity that takes pleasure in suffering and consists of nothing but struggle and endless suffering. Nor do we proclaim a Christianity for naïve optimists who are more credulous than credible. We proclaim Christ, the one who was crucified and rose from the dead. Otherwise it would be a form of mutilation both for us and for those to whom we hand on our faith, which is the faith of the Church.

4. *The hour of Jesus holds the victorious power of the Holy Spirit working in us*

We must also try at least to touch upon this phenomenon of the "trial of faith". How can we go about doing that? Let us have the courage not to use any other method (for example, sociology, psychology) than the one that will allow us to enter into the reality of the trial of faith *through the categories of the mystery of God and of the faith.*

Therefore we have the courage to fix our eyes on Jesus, whose ministry began with a trial—with the temptation in the desert. On Golgotha the supreme trial took place: "Come down from the cross!" In the desert he did not abandon his messianic plan; on Golgotha he did not forsake his Cross. He commended himself entirely to his Father; truly he committed his spirit into his hands (Lk 23:46).

Between these two trials we find the mysterious night of Gethsemane (see Mt 26:36–56). The hours of Jesus' agony and struggle contain the hours of trial of all the just in the history of salvation, including the hour of our testing, along with all the trials and all the torments of those who are "tested"—with the exception of sin (see Heb 4:15). Moreover, Jesus' Hour holds the victorious power of the Holy Spirit—for our sake.

How much light will be shed by the darkness of this great, enduring night upon the darkness of our nights, which begin over and over again?

5. *"Thy will be done"*

Let us choose as our guide, our "mystagogue", who will lead us into the mystery of Gethsemane, Cardinal Wojtyla, since he served in that capacity during the retreat that he gave at the Vatican in 1976. We will cite only one passage:

> This prayer is in fact a meeting between the human will of Jesus Christ and the eternal will of God, which at this moment can be seen as the will of the Father concerning his Son. The Son had become man in order that this meeting might express

all the truth of the human will and the human heart, anxious to escape the evil and the suffering, the condemnation and the scourging, the crown of thorns, the cross and death (cf. Mk 14:43–15:33). He had become man in order that this truth might then serve to reveal all the grandeur of the love that expresses itself in a "gift of oneself", in sacrifice: "God loved the world so much that he sacrificed his only-begotten Son" (Jn 3:16). In this hour that "eternal love" (Jer 31) has to give proof of itself by the sacrifice of a human heart. And it does indeed give proof of itself! The Son does not shrink from giving his own heart, for it to become an altar, a place of complete self-abnegation even before the cross was to serve that purpose (cf. Jn 19:34).

The human will, the will of the man meets the will of God. The human will speaks by means of the heart and expresses the human truth: "If it be possible may this cup pass me by" (Mt 26:39). But at the same time the human will surrenders itself to the will of God, as if passing beyond the human truth, beyond the cry of the heart; it is as if it were taking unto itself not only the eternal judgment of the Father and the Son in the Holy Spirit, but also the power that flows from God, from the will of God, from the God who is love (cf. 1 Jn 4:8). Christ leaves behind, so to speak, this Love which so often has gone before the cry of the heart, and says: "Nevertheless, not my will, but thine, be done" (Lk 22:42).

All prayer is a meeting between the human will and the will of God; for this we are indebted to the Son's obedience to the Father: "Your will be done" (Lk 22:42). And obedience does not mean only renunciation of one's own will; it means opening one's spiritual eyes and ears to the love which is God himself, God who loved the world so much that for its sake he sacrificed his only-begotten Son (Jn 3:16). "Here is the man" (Jn 19:5). After his prayer in Gethsemane, Jesus Christ, the Son of God, rises to his feet fortified: fortified by the obedience (Phil 2:8; Heb 5:8) which has enabled him once again to attain to Love, as gift from the Father for the world (cf. Jn 17:18; 1 Jn 3:1; 4:16) and for all mankind. He rises to his feet and goes back to his disciples.[2]

6. *The obedience of faith*

We know what Jesus said when he emerged from the Hour of Gethsemane and what happened afterward. But it is precisely *in the strength of this entire Paschal Mystery* that we are capable of entering into "our own hours", so as to participate in his victory after participating in his suffering.

In the documents of Vatican II there is a passage that helps us to understand this mystery. It is found in the Constitution on Divine Revelation: "'The obedience of faith' (Rom 16:26; cf. Rom 1:5; 2 Cor 10:5–6) must be given to God as he reveals himself. By faith man freely commits his entire self to God, making the full submission of his intellect and will to God who reveals, and willingly assenting to the Revelation given by him" (*Dei Verbum* 5).

From God's perspective, revelation is actually an opening in Jesus Christ. The God of creation *opens himself*, so to speak, to man in Christ as the God of salvation. Moreover, the "opening" to man indicates an involvement in and a commitment to the destiny of mankind. "For, by his incarnation, ... the Son of God has in a certain way united himself with each man. He worked with human hands, he thought with a human mind. He acted with a human will, and with a human heart he loved. Born of the Virgin

---

[2] *The Sign of Contradiction* (New York: Seabury Press, 1979), pp. 149–50.

Mary, he has truly been made one of us, like to us in all things except sin (*Gaudium et spes*, 22)." God therefore has spoken and "has given himself" in Jesus Christ to the end, and he did this in the sight of man and for his sake.

Now it is up to man to respond to this revelation of God. The gift of God makes demands and creates obligations, but it does not coerce. Man's dignity and freedom remain intact. The gift is a call to take a stance, one that is in keeping with the gift of God. To the total gift of God there is only one response: *the total gift of man*. Man places himself entirely at God's disposal. It is a question not only of accepting a message, but also of giving assent to a new vocation and to a new meaning of one's life. In this supernatural dimension the grace of God and the help of the Holy Spirit are necessary. For the children of God "were born, not of blood nor of the will of the flesh nor of the will of man, but of God" (Jn 1:13). Man is reborn of water and the Spirit (cf. Jn 3:3–5).

He becomes "a new creation" (cf., for example, 2 Cor 5:17), so new that it must be called by another name.

This is what makes up the "obedience of faith", which is not linked to any one faculty of the soul, but goes deeper, to the very structure of the human person and his dynamism. In this "place" we confront a unique potential for being enriched in the faith; but at that same place the faith is exposed to all sorts of wounds and weaknesses.

7. *To obey the call is to keep taking risks*

When we say that the disciples *listened* to Christ, we mean that they were able to *obey* his call. *How are we to obey*, when this paramount Value overturns a hierarchy of previously acquired values, when it abolishes them, when it questions them, when the new world of faith positively threatens us with a loss of our being. To obey, then, means to keep taking risks.

The pages of salvation history are full of descriptions of trying events. So it is with the pages being written by our generation.

What occurred in the soul of the scribe who decided to follow Jesus—and learned that the latter had no place to lay his head? What was he thinking, the disciple who was hesitating between the Lord and his dead father (cf. Mt 8:19–22)? And what happened to Peter, who was tempted and a tempter, when he rebuked Jesus for announcing salvation through the Cross (see Mt 16:22), when he defended him with a sword (see Mt 26:51), and when he defended himself by denying Jesus (see Mt 26:69 ff.)? And what went on in the hearts of the unhappy disciples when he said to them, "Will you also go away?" (Jn 6:67), or in the hearts of those who, after doubting Jesus, met their risen hope along the road to Emmaus (Lk 24:13–35)?

After considering these human dramas, do we not have to return to the Heart of the God-man at the hour of Gethsemane? Truly, during this trial was accomplished the insertion of the Eternal Wisdom into the dimensions of human knowledge, practical intelligence, and feelings. Eternal Love enclosed itself within the dimensions of that Heart, which could not contain it and consequently seemed to burst.[3]

8. *In confident faith . . . , the night begins to perceive the "rising of the dawn"*

My dear friends, allow me to forgo presenting an analysis of the particular forms taken by the trials of faith in the

[3] Ibid.

province of reason, trials that proceed, for example, from different views of man and of reality, or in the province of values, resulting, for instance, from various ethical concepts or even from the problem of innocent suffering. One magnificent passage by John Paul II encompasses them all: this hymn to Saint John of the Cross, intoned in Segovia, contains striking stanzas about our time.

> Despite his conquests, modern man, in his personal and collective experience, sometimes skirts the abyss of abandonment, the temptation to nihilism, the absurdity of so much physical, moral, and spiritual suffering. The dark night, the proof that puts us into contact with the mystery of evil and demands the openness of the faith, sometimes assumes epochal dimensions and communal proportions.
>
> Even the Christian and the Church herself can find themselves identified with the Christ of Saint John of the Cross, at the height of his sorrow and abandonment. All of these sufferings have been taken up by Christ in his cry of sorrow and in his trusting abandonment of himself to the Father. In faith, hope, and love, the night is transformed into day, suffering into joy, death into life.
>
> John of the Cross, through his own experience, invites us to be confident, to allow ourselves to be purified by God; in confident, loving faith, the night begins to perceive "the rising of the dawn". It becomes luminous as an Easter night—"O blessed night!", "O night fairer than the dawn!"—and announces the Resurrection and the victory, the coming of the Bridegroom who joins the Christian to himself, "the Beloved Bride transformed in the Beloved Bridegroom".
>
> May the dark nights that come over individual consciences and the communities of our time be enlivened in pure faith; in the hope "that obtains as much as it hopes for"; in the ardent love of the Spirit's strength, so that they might be transformed into bright days for our suffering

humanity, in the victory of the Risen One who sets cap-
tives free by the power of his Cross!

Thus spoke John Paul II.

9. *"Witnessing is nothing other than professing"*

I cannot conclude with that, because I am concerned about
responding to the challenge of *our* times. Just as faith leads
to witness, so too we do not have the right to remain silent
about *the testing of faith in the situation of giving witness.* Just
as in the development of faith, the moment in which a
person commends himself to God is the most vulnerable,
so too *in the life of faith the most vulnerable moment is the
passage from faith to witness.*

   Christian witness is the product—ever new and always
concrete—of an encounter in which God reveals himself,
and man, entrusting himself to God in faith, becomes *at the
same time a sharer in salvation and an active participant in it.*

   To believe is to *accept* the witness of God himself. To
believe means also *to take up God's witness and to express it by
one's own witness.* "Witnessing" is nothing other than "professing": the witness to Christ is the one who professes faith
in him. Very often the "profession" is made in the midst of
fears, trials, sufferings, or persecutions: "fighting without
and fear within" (2 Cor 7:5). Witness is, indeed, *a new form
of gift,* full of various benefits, both external and spiritual,
even as far as the sacrifice of one's life.

   Christ is terribly clear: "You shall be my witnesses"
(Acts 1:8); "Every one who acknowledges me before men,
I also will acknowledge before my Father who is in heaven"
(Mt 10:32). This is the "faithful witness" speaking (Rev 3:14).
The witness who, after the battle, after the agony in

Gethsemane, went to bear witness: "For this I was born, and for this I have come into the world, to bear witness to the truth" (Jn 18:37). Henceforth all the testimonies given by the disciples of Christ are borne up by the victorious power of the Cross and bear the marks of that struggle.

I am thinking of those brothers and sisters who are kept away from witnessing by a trial of their faith that is like an intervening spiritual space. Is it possible to give witness and at the same time to undergo trials? Yes, as the following examples demonstrate: the decision to be married in the Church, or to have one's child baptized and to raise him in the faith (catechesis), attending Mass, taking a stand in matters of faith, morality, the Church or man—whether it be during a conversation, in a pastoral letter or a homily, or when faced with a decision that will affect one's entire life.

This interior, spiritual space is somehow defined—this is precisely why it is a *trial*. It may be defined by a danger, a threat, by doubts about the reliability of one's own motives, which may be affected by public opinion, popularity, physical or psychological coercion or violence. The fundamental risk to be taken in faith, namely, *the gift of oneself to God*, reappears in each concrete situation.

Peter and John, two of Jesus' first disciples, spent a night in prison; thus a time of trial preceded the first public stand taken in the history of the Church, namely, with regard to the question: "Is it right in the sight of God to listen to you rather than to God? ... [W]e cannot but speak of what we have seen and heard" (Acts 4:19–20). And what sort of dark night did Saint Maximilian Kolbe experience in the concentration camp in Auschwitz before giving his testimony to Love during roll call, before giving his life for his brother; what did he experience in the starvation bunker, where he held out to the end, faithful to his witness?

10. *The Church defends the freedom of human consciences*

What will the Church do? How will she help her brothers
and sisters to get through the time of trial, to go across that
space while following Jesus? How is she to help the mil-
lions of people on all continents, wherever freedom of religion is endangered and also where it is safeguarded?

Faithful to Christ, the Redeemer of man, *the Church defends
the freedom of human consciences!* Let everything that goes on
between God and man take place in freedom from all exterior constraints and from every threat. The controversies
between religion, agnosticism, and atheism should not
infringe on the freedom of human consciences.

In his speech to the representatives of the United Nations
on October 2, 1979, John Paul II declared, following the
teaching of Vatican II, that the confrontation between the
religious understanding of the world and the agnostic or
atheistic world view—which is one of the "signs of the
times"—can take place within humane, honest, and respect-
ful limits, without any need to attack the essential rights of
the conscience of each and every man and woman in the
world.

The Church *helps* her brothers and sisters by imitating
the first Christian community of Jerusalem: the Acts of
the Apostles tell us that the *earnest prayer* of the Church
went up to God unceasingly on behalf of Peter, who was
in prison (Acts 12:5). Do not leave me alone, said Christ
to his apostles (see Jn 16:32). Do not leave our brothers
and sisters alone when they must undergo the trial of
witnessing—perhaps in our midst. Another thing that can
assist them is *the witness* of those who already (or perhaps
again?) have the opportunity to give witness, whether indi-
vidually or collectively. Thus a supernatural atmosphere is

produced, resulting in support for those who are being "tested". Do not leave your brother and your sister alone— look, they are perhaps right beside you. . . .

My dear friends! Let us remain faithful to this principle: that we need to speak about the trials of faith in the light of faith. We wish to conclude with the following prayer:

> *Come, O Holy Spirit, come!*
> *And from your celestial home*
> *Shed a ray of light divine.*
>
> *Come, O Father of the poor!*
> *Come, O source of all our store!*
> *Come, within our bosoms shine!*
>
> . . .
>
> *In our labor, rest most sweet;*
> *Grateful coolness in the heat;*
> *Solace in the midst of woe.*
>
> *O most blessed Light divine,*
> *Shine within these hearts of thine,*
> *And our inmost being fill.*

Reflection by Jacques Guillet, S.J.

The text of the conference by Franciszek Cardinal Macharski needs no commentary; from start to finish it is simple
and direct. But it is profound and far-reaching, which is
why it gives us food for thought and points for meditation.
Here we would simply like to highlight several of the main
themes of this text and to demonstrate their internal coherence, rooted as they are in the Word of God and Christian
revelation.

1. *Freedom and faith*

The entire conference is centered on the call to freedom,
or, more precisely, on the fight for freedom. This theme
resounds from the very first sentence: "The test of faith is
the fight for freedom...." (§ 1). It dominates the whole
concluding section: "The Church defends the freedom of
human consciences! Let everything that goes on between
God and man take place in freedom from all exterior constraints ..." (§ 10). We know, we sense from afar, how urgent
this battle is for the Archbishop of Krakow, but even though
this intense battle concerns all human consciences on every
continent, it is above all for Christians a battle waged in
faith, a trial of faith.

The relationship between freedom and faith is not defined
anywhere explicitly. It is perceived as something self-
evident, and if this self-evident character seems more remote
to us in the West, it is because, being accustomed to many

freedoms, we do not adequately grasp the extent to which faith is an experience of freedom or the fact that faith is necessary in order to win freedom. We must not forget that an entire people is currently living through what the Cardinal only begins to suggest.

2. *The night of faith*

The theme of faith put to the test, in contrast, recurs several times, practically on each page. Here there is no longer any need to be discreet, and the memories crowd each other: Abraham, Isaac, Jacob, Moses, Mary, and Jesus (§ 2). These names are only mentioned; the only trial that is developed at greater length is the night of Gethsemane. It is supposed that some Christians will know what it meant to Abraham to set out for an unknown world, the long wait for a promise that increasingly appeared to be illusory, and the shock he experienced when God seemed to demand back the son he had just given him. All the children of Abraham ought to know this story, which is theirs. What is touching is precisely the tone that the speaker assumes here: "With what reverence we pronounce the names of our Fathers in faith. . . ."

One word occurs more than once to describe the trial of faith: it is a night. The influence of the mystics, particularly of Saint John of the Cross, is evident. Moreover it is openly acknowledged, and the Cardinal goes on to cite at length the beautiful passage in which John Paul II, during his trip to Segovia, compared the nights of the great Spanish mystic and the nights that mankind is living through today (§§ 2, 8).

In this juxtaposition there is much more than a clever comparison: there is a profound truth, namely, that the trial of faith is of a spiritual order, that it strikes man "at the juncture between flesh and spirit", that it always appears to be a threat to all our most essential values, and that it always involves a new risk (§ 7).

This theme is one of the main points of the conference (§§ 4 and 5). But the manner in which it is developed is surprising. Even though this is constantly verified by the spiritual experience of the saints and that of humanity, the focus here is on the person of Jesus Christ and the mystery of Gethsemane. Franciszek Macharski has not forgotten Pascal among those who testify to the night.

What is revealed in the mystery of the Agony in the Garden is the encounter between the human will and the will of God, between man's heart, with all the desires and suffering he bears within it, and the Love of God. The last thing Jesus says [there], "Not my will, but yours, be done" (Lk 22:42), "does not mean only renunciation of one's own will; it means opening one's spiritual eyes and ears to the love which is God himself" (§ 5). This is a decisive statement: beyond obedience and submission to the will that has been acknowledged, there is a movement whereby Christ's human will collapses and abandons itself in the Father's Love.

Now this mystery is repeated in the obedience of faith (§ 6). For man, too, it is a question of accepting his new vocation and the meaning God wishes to give to his life. The point is that the hour of Gethsemane, this moment in the story of Jesus, is at the heart of every human story. It is the revelation of the mystery of the Son of God made man, "the insertion of the Eternal Wisdom into the dimensions of human knowledge, practical intelligence, and feelings" (§ 7). Everything in Christ's life, all

that he does, all that he suffers, he lives for us. This is
another aspect of the faith and its testing: it is communication, fellowship.

3. *The communication of the faith*

The test of faith and the communication of the faith: that is
the two-part title of the conference, and communication is
in fact the first of the two to be mentioned. This is, no
doubt, in order to emphasize better the connection with
the overall theme, "handing on the faith today". Although
we are dealing with it here in second place, that does not
mean it has become secondary or marginal. On the contrary, it is present everywhere and recurs in almost every
paragraph. Whereas the "test" or "trial" forms the central
block of material, "communication" accompanies every step
of the development. Moreover it is present under various
aspects.

The first aspect to appear is that of communion. The
trial of faith binds us together with all those who have experienced it before us and for us, "our Fathers in faith, whose
trials merited faith for us" (§ 2). Let not the word "merit"
cause grumblers to furrow their brows; the context shows
that here we are dealing with that "cloud of witnesses" who
surround us (Heb 12:1) so as to defend us against sin. There
is no question of detracting anything at all from the unique
mediation of Jesus Christ. Yet the entire conference attempts
to highlight the connection between the trial and the
communication.

At the root of this connection is the trial of Jesus,
from the temptation in the desert to Golgotha, and at
the heart of that trial is the night in Gethsemane. "The
hours of Jesus' agony and struggle contain the hours of

trial of all the just in the history of salvation, including the hour of our testing, along with all the trials ... of those who are 'tested'" (§ 4). The Cardinal is acquainted with Pascal, but he does not need to cite *The Mystery of Jesus* in order to express an essential point of the Christian faith. If "Christ died for our sins" (1 Cor 15:3), if he died "for my brother", even the weakest one, as Paul reminded the Christians of Corinth (1 Cor 8:11), he could not have died without knowing what he did and why he was giving up his life. Without this connection, this bond that originates with him, we are not saved by him, we owe him nothing, and we can do nothing to unite ourselves to him.

This essential connection between the night of Jesus and our nights will recur several times. We note here two convergent sources of inspiration. On the one hand, there are the great intuitions of Vatican II: "By his incarnation, ... the Son of God has in a certain way united himself with each man" (*Gaudium et spes*, no. 22; § 6). And then there is the experience of our times, the experience of a world crushed by its sufferings, tempted by nihilism, lost in absurdity (§ 8). It is, if we dare say it, a sorrowful and precious acquisition of our age: this discovery of a true affinity between the spiritual trials of the saints and the desert paths that mankind, bereft of God and overwhelmed with horrors, must traverse in the night. Though seemingly a paradox, it does not surprise the disciple of the Gospel. Jesus' paths, the paths of his temptation and of his forty days in the desert, brought him directly to the sinners and the publicans, to the sinful women and prostitutes. That is where the sick people are; that is where the power of God restores life to those who were dead.

4. *Witness and confession*

The conference ends with a paragraph on witness and confession, which summarizes the preceding lines. To believe
is an act of communion, since it is accepting the testimony,
the witness of God himself. Therefore it means taking seriously God's commitment, the step by which he entrusts
himself to man's assent. To believe is an act of freedom:
faith—the movement of adhering to a personal being, to
the personal gift of God—can never be imposed from without. The commandment, "you shall love" not only presupposes freedom ("you shall choose to love"), but also awakens
that freedom by requiring man to withdraw to the central
place within himself, to that point in his heart where man
makes decisions about his life.

To believe is also an act of communication. It is recog-
nizing God's call and responding to it; it is giving him access
to the heart of our existence. It is also a communication
with men. That is why the faith is witnessing and professing (§ 9). It is witnessing, inasmuch as it is addressed to the
heart of the onlooker. Neither words nor promises nor explanations are capable of arousing faith. The faith can only
spring from the heart, and the heart awakens only to the
beat of a living heart. This living heart can be, and always
is, at bottom, the heart of the Son of God made man. But
it can also be the heart of the witness, the one who by his
life and his actions shows that his heart is enthralled.

The testimony that the Cardinal has in mind is the one
that so often awaits today's Christian, the witness given in
difficult times, in the solitude of the night. The theme of
the night returns here in full force. The point is that authentic Christian witness is not the triumphant affirmation of a
courage capable of confronting all dangers. It is, rather, the

witness that Christ's disciples give in the hollow of their weakness, "in my infirmities", as Saint Paul used to say. It is the hour in which they "are borne up by the victorious power of the Cross and bear the marks of that struggle" (§ 9). What Cardinal Macharski emphasizes about the example of Saint Maximilian Kolbe in the Auschwitz concentration camp is not primarily the heroic gesture of the Franciscan confronting the S.S. officers during roll call; it is his hidden witness, which he continued to give until the end in the starvation bunker.